GOD IS GOD

and

We are NOT!

By BARBARA VOLZ

GOD IS GOD

and

We are NOT!

Surely I will set you free,
for purposes of good!
Jeremiah 15:11

By BARBARA VOLZ

GOD IS GOD and We are NOT!

By Barbara Volz

Copyright © 1995, 1999 and 2002

Requests for information should be addressed to:

Match Made in Heaven Publishing
P. O. Box 220
Dana Point, CA 92629
(800)-445-8404

ISBN 1-929921-01-2

Scripture taken from the **New American Standard Bible,** Copyright © 1960, 1962, 1963, 1968, 1973, 1974, 1977 by the Lockman Foundation and are used by permission.

Dedicated to

JESUS

My Lover, Savior and Friend

CONTENTS

FOREWORD
Jerry, Cripples DO Walk.. 1
The Journey Into MORE.. 4
A WORD TO SINGLES... 7
THE WALKING OF IT... 11
A True LOVE STORY.. 23
GET YOUR HOUSE IN ORDER.. 28
Editorial Update... 36
THE SOVEREIGNTY OF GOD.. 37
LIVE IN HOUSES YOU DIDN'T BUILD.. 42
MIKALA'S recollection of GRANDPA'S SAYINGS........... 50
DO YOU...WANT TO BE FREE?... 51
BROKENNESS '101'... 55
QUIT BEGGING FOR CURSES. 61
MARRIAGE...BATTLEGROUND or BLESSING?............. 65
THE DEFILED BRIDE... 74
HEAVEN BUILT FOR ONE?... 77
NO SUPERSTARS (Can I Be Your Donkey, Lord?)......... 80
CHAINED TO THINGS?... 85
THE CHRISTMAS ISSUE... 91
LET'S GET SAVED, CHURCH.. 95
WHERE YOUR TREASURE IS... 107
FAITH, The Battle is the Lord's... 113
MY COLORS WILL BE CLEAR.. 119
PASTORS and MINISTERS.. 120

FOREWORD

My prayer is that God use this book to minister LIFE into the depths of your innermost being. LIFE into your soul. Life into your call. That He restore your hope and give you HIS vision for your life.

"Where there is no vision, the people perish." (Proverbs 29:18)

This book will take you into the **walking it out** of the Christian lifestyle. To walk with God. To hear His voice. To do what He says.

One of the questions people ask me is, "How did you learn to hear God's voice?"

My response is, "We all hear someone's voice; it just depends on which voice we listen to—the voices or THE VOICE?"

The word God gave to Jeremiah is a place you can begin:

If you return, then I will restore you
before Me you will stand
And if you extract the precious from the worthless
you will become My spokesman.
They for their part may turn to you
But as for you, you must not turn to them.
(Jeremiah 15:19)

This book will give you new life. It will compel you to go forth in victory.

May God abundantly bless you into all that He is.

Barbara

Jerry...Cripples DO Walk

At the age of thirty-five, as I sat before the doctor at the MDA clinic, he confirmed the word that I'd been hearing for five years. "You have Charcot-Marie-Tooth, the tests are complete and positive. You know the progression of the disease and that there is no treatment or cure." The prognosis was grim at best; you simply wither away. I knew it well. I'd seen it in my own family from an early age. My dad wasn't like the other dads, and my aunt didn't seem normal either. As I grew from a child to a woman I'd watched Muscular Dystrophy plague our family.

Charcot-Marie-Tooth—what's that, you ask? It's a form of Muscular Atrophy. I'd heard for years that two of daddy's four kids would get it; that it's inherited. Years later, here I was, receiving the same diagnosis my dad had gotten 33 years earlier. I'd spent the last five years progressively getting weaker physically and going to the MDA clinic in Little Rock, where they had been charting my decline through various tests and muscle biopsies to see how much muscle I had left. I'd been on the Jerry Lewis Telethon each Labor Day helping raise money to find a cure. Finally, with no hope in sight, I went to the MDA research center at Columbia Presbyterian Medical Center in New York City.

The Doctor finished his analysis of the situation.

Then, a most startling thing happened. I was sitting there listening to the doctor and suddenly; I had a vision of Jesus. He appeared, above the doctor, and looked down at me and said, "Barbara, when are you just going to trust ME?" His words were simple, but they pierced my heart.

I stood and said to the doctor, "God's going to heal me. I'm going home, no more tests."

He looked at me and laughed.

I went back to the hotel, checked out, and headed home to tell my doctors in Little Rock, Arkansas the same thing.

"No more tests...God's going to heal me." Same reaction. They laughed.

I'd never had a vision before. No one had told me that "those things" still happened, you know...the book of Acts stuff. (Acts 2:17, 10:3-17, and 16:9) But I'd seen God's face, his words were clear. So, I **spoke** the word concerning my situation. I made the declaration that God was going to heal me. I'd gotten that in the spirit when I saw the Lord. Now I spoke it by faith. *"Death and life are in the power of the tongue." (Proverbs 18:21)*

Back at home, the Lord said, "Start walking."
"God, this is killing me," I said.
"You're dying anyway; just do what I said," he replied.

The Bible speaks in *1 Corinthians 12:6-11* of the gifts of the Holy Spirit and two of them are, "the working of miracles and the gift of healing."

Don't wonder about this "God speaking to me" stuff. Jesus said in *John 10:27, "My sheep hear My voice, and I know them, and they follow Me."* I heard God's voice and I started walking, and I walked and walked and walked...

One month later, **I RAN all the way home from my walk.** Praise God!

I got to call Jerry Lewis, who's of Jewish descent, and tell him that I wouldn't be on the telethon that year because, by Jesus' stripes, I was healed. (See *Isaiah 53:5 and I Peter 2:24*.)

After I was healed I had to re-evaluate everything that I'd come to know as life. Before, it had only extended as far as my withering muscles and hope could take me. My fears had eaten up my faith. Now, I'd met a God so big that the word He spoke activated my faith. Now, it was just a matter of **walking** it out.

Do you know about faith? The Bible says, *"The righteous man will live by his faith" (Habakkuk 2:4, Romans 1:17)*.

Jesus said, *"Daughter, your faith has made you well; go in peace, and be healed of your affliction" (Mark 5:34, also Mark 10:52)*.

Jesus also said in *Luke 18:8, "When the Son of Man comes, will He find faith on the earth?"*

"Whatever is not from faith is sin" (Romans 14:23).

Do you know what the word of God is over your life? It's the HOLY BIBLE; that's the word over your life.

Isaiah 55:11 says, *"So shall My word be which goes forth from My mouth; it shall not return to me empty,*

Jerry, Cripples DO Walk

without accomplishing what I desire, and without succeeding in the matter for which I sent it."

Jesus also said, *"Heaven and earth will pass away, but My words shall not pass away" (Matthew 24:35).*

Jesus spoke the word over Peter, *"When you grow old, you will stretch out your hands, and someone else will gird you, and bring you where you do not wish to go" (John 21:18).*

In *Acts 12* is the story of James being put to death and Peter being arrested. You'll read that after his arrest he fell asleep between two guards, bound with chains. He wasn't an old man yet, so he didn't fear for his life...he just got some rest.

An interesting note to my miraculous healing. A friend of mine had gone through a divorce a couple of years earlier and left the church I'd been a member of most of my life. She'd found shelter in a spirit-filled church that taught the whole Bible...you know, that God still has a people doing the stuff Jesus did. As I would run into her over the years, she'd always say the same thing. "Barbara, I'm praying for you and God's going to heal you."

I always gave her the same answer, "Joyce, I've told you, this is inherited and two of us kids are supposed to have it."

She would always reply, "I'm not going to quit praying, the Bible says that by Jesus' stripes we ARE healed."

Years later, when I went back to Little Rock, I asked God if I could see Joyce and let her know that He had healed me. I ran into her at the mall and said, "Look, Joyce, I'm healed."

She said, "I never quit praying."

The question is, who's "walking" on your prayers?

All it takes is one person to STAND in faith. *Ezekiel 22:30* says, *"And I searched for a man among them who should build up the wall and stand in the gap before Me for the land, that I should not destroy it."*

Will you be the one to stand in the gap for your land, wherever it is?

The final word in this chapter is...it's been 17 years and no one in our family has gotten this disease. Praise God, the curse is broken and we've escaped.

The Journey into MORE

I was healed. I went to church praising God and I was met with unbelief. What? No crutches? How can that be? God doesn't heal today!

But I WAS WALKING and standing strong in my newfound faith. Why didn't anyone "get it?"

Finally, I asked the lady at the Christian Bookstore if she had any information on this kind of thing? She gave me a tape on healing and invited me to a healing seminar that weekend.

I went, and I watched. John, the minister in charge, began by sharing his testimony. As a young man, he'd been in a major band. A friend told him about the love of Jesus. He asked Jesus to come into his heart and forgive him of his sins. Then the friend gave him a Bible, told him to read it, and invited him to go to church on Sunday.

After the Sunday service his friend got up to leave expecting John to follow. As he continued sitting in the pew, his friend said, "John, come on, it's over, let's go.

John asked, "How can it be over? When do we get to do the stuff?"

"What stuff?" his friend questioned.

"The stuff Jesus did. You know, heal the sick, raise the dead...the stuff that was in the book you told me to read." *(Read Matthew 10:5-8, Mark 16:15-20.)*

"Oh, John, that stuff doesn't happen anymore," his friend replied.

At that, John, the new convert, assured his friend that since the Bible said that those things happen, they still must.

>Jesus said, *"He who believes in Me, the works that I do shall he do also; and greater works than these shall he do; because I go to the Father"* (John 14:12).

>*Jesus Christ is the same yesterday and today, yes and forever."* (Hebrews 13:8)

With that, John proceeded to go out and pray for the sick.

The Journey into MORE

I sat at the healing seminar, listening and trying to be receptive to these new things. I saw legs grow out, people get out of wheelchairs, miracles of all sorts. The experience definitely challenged a lifetime of "religion." These things were happening through the gifts and the workings of the Holy Spirit *(1 Corinthians 12:4-10)* of which I knew nothing.

The next day, a woman came into my store. She was a GOOD customer, the store was full of people, and the phone had been ringing incessantly...then GOD started, "Barbara, pray for her."

"Lord, I'm not sure that stuff works and I'm surely not sure it works through me."

"Barbara, pray for her."

"Lord, I'm not sure that stuff works and I'm surely not sure it works through me. Besides, Lord, she's a REALLY good customer, the store is full of people, and don't you hear the phone ringing? God - PLEASE."

"BARBARA, PRAY FOR HER."

"Becky, I have to pray for you," I said in surrender.

I don't have a clue what I prayed that day, all I know was that she cried and then she left.

The next time I saw Becky was six months later. She shared that she had been a closet alcoholic and addicted to prescription drugs for ten years and was preparing to commit suicide; but she felt the need to come to my athletic store to buy her daughter a pair of Reeboks first. Through the prayer that day, she said that God delivered her of her addictions and suicide...she could face tomorrow now. To God be the glory.

I didn't know anything about her personal life, all I knew was that GOD said, "PRAY FOR HER."

GOD IS GOD and We are NOT!

As I was preparing this chapter, I called Becky for permission to share her story, and ask her for her recollection of that day, which was the beginning of my PRAY FOR HER walk.

Becky shared that she had been high as a kite that day. She had gone to the grocery store to get some things, dropped her sack, and just driven off without it.

You see, only Becky and God knew that she had been on a ten-year self-destruct course of sleeping pills and alcohol. She had also been having back pains, which the doctor said could be from gall bladder, liver, or ulcer problems. As she shared this news with her husband; Becky said, "I probably have cirrhosis of the liver."

He immediately replied, "You don't drink THAT much."

"Yes I do, you just don't know."

No one knew, only God and Becky. God also knew what it took to deliver her from the path of destruction. As always, God has the goods and He knows where His kids live. He also knows just how far we have to go before we are ready to look up. Becky had a divine appointment with her God at my store that day and was healed, delivered, and SET FREE.

Thank you God...for your anointing that breaks the yokes.

Jesus said, 2,000 years ago, *"The Spirit of the Lord is upon Me, because He anointed Me to preach the gospel to the poor. He has sent Me to proclaim release to the captives, and recovery of sight to the blind, to set free those who are downtrodden. To proclaim the favorable year of the Lord (Luke 4:18-19).*

That's what our Savior did and what He left for us to do...
Let's be doing it.

A WORD TO SINGLES

Be About Your FATHER'S Business, and all these things will be added to you.

At this time in my life, I was a single mom of two teen-agers; Paul and Mikala. As far as my walk, I'd learned beyond a shadow of a doubt that God has called us to be holy, even as He is holy (*Romans 12:1*). That issue was settled, and for me, I knew I would not tempt God by dating. It was a time in my life when God set me apart to Himself to heal me, to deliver me, and to set me free.

I believe it is imperative for singles to have this time of restoration with God.

One day, as a divorcee, I was under my house redoing the ductwork, and couldn't figure it out. I couldn't even find my tin snips when I needed them. In utter frustration, I cried out, "Daddy, where are you when I need you?"

The voice of my loving heavenly Father answered so clearly, "Barbara, I'm taking you on now - you've got no one else to blame. You got rid of Paul (ex-husband), I took your daddy (he had just died), now - all you have is ME and I'M TAKING YOU ON."

"Oh, Lord."

After my healing I was sure there must be more to God than I was aware of. I'd grown up in a denominational church, taught Sunday School, tithed, did the things I thought were right...so what happened? Through the divorce and all the judgments that went with it, I'd told God, "IF that's what You are - I don't want You."

I was in for the surprise of my life; THAT wasn't God at all. He led me to a spirit-filled church where I cried because the Holy Spirit was allowed to come in, touching and healing God's kids - hearts, minds, bodies, and souls. The ministry team women prayed for me and I'd cry. I'd get into messes; they'd pray for me and I'd cry. Those women were filled with the Holy Ghost and had walked the walk of holiness and dedication to Almighty God.

Through the months and years, God was healing me of all the stuff that made me do the things I did. He showed me His love, unconditionally. I wanted what those people had. I wanted to be filled with the Holy Spirit, to have the God of the Universe living inside me, to walk in communion with my God as they did. Having life to live, and life to give.

I figured it shouldn't be that hard to get the Holy Ghost; after all, I had a triple Master's degree, so this surely wouldn't be a problem. Oh well, **GOD IS GOD and We are NOT!** He is HOLY and He comes into holy vessels; so HE was turning up the heat and burning EVERYTHING out of my life that couldn't stand the fire. Trust me, God knows just how hot the fire has to be to burn everything out that stands between you and Him. Yes, it's tough dying to life as you know it for the higher call but…God NEVER said it would be easy; He said that He would be with us.

A counselor friend decided that since I was game I could be her guinea pig at a weekend retreat for spirit-filled women. Well, here goes this kid who'd always been taught against the gifts and the workings of the Holy Spirit - packed with all my religion and the *"tradition of the elders, that makes the word of God of no effect." (*Refer to *Mark 7:6-8* and *2 Timothy 3:5.)* You see, in my church, we'd made fun of THOSE people.

During the ministry time, Faye taught the women by example. She put me in the circle to be prayed for. As she prayed in the Spirit, the Lord showed her the root of the problem. She asked me if I would share what I was experiencing with the ladies.

I was seeing a vision of when I was about two-years-old and was checking on Daddy to see if he was OK, because he had Muscular Dystrophy and we never knew when he would die, so I would always check on him.

Faye, sensing that God was healing me of my fears and fear of love, asked me to finish the story.

"Well, when I went back into the room, Jesus was holding Daddy in His arms and everything was OK."

You see, Daddy always taught us his Marine Corps philosophy; that if you never get close to anyone, then it won't hurt you when they die. I suppose he was trying to prepare us for his death, however, God honored a little girl's prayers and kept my dad alive until I was thirty-five-years old.

A Word to Singles

Later, I began to receive my prayer language; however, I only got ONE word. God was surely using the foolishness of the gospel to confound the wisdom of the wise *(1 Corinthians 1:18-31)*. I thought, surely, I'd have languages. Oh, what utter pride! **GOD IS GOD** and He's going to do it HIS way. WHEN you are faithful in little, you're given much *(Matthew 25:21-30)*.

It seems there are two problems in the counseling field:
1. Single, wanting to be married.
2. Married, wanting to be single.

However, there's a place the Lord wants to take His children. The one Paul spoke of in *Philippians 4:11-13:*

Not that I speak from want; for I have learned to be content in whatever circumstances I am. I know how to get along with humble means, and I also know how to live in prosperity; in any and every circumstance I have learned the secret of being filled and going hungry, both of having abundance and suffering need. I can do ALL things through Him who strengthens me.

Singles—you will only get someone as healthy as you are…you get what you play for. If you die to the flesh, and won't play games with hell for a flesh fix, God can send you a holy man or woman who has walked that path also. Remember that two halves don't make a whole. If you can't live without someone, you'll never have what it takes to live with them. Jesus has to be enough. Then He can bless, and one day, when you least expect it God Almighty joins two hands together at His throne. Be healthy enough not to be so desperate that you choose a "project," but to wait until God says you are each ready for the blessing He has for you. Remember the widow at Zarephath *(1 Kings 17:9-16)*. One day earlier, she wouldn't have been so desperate. One day later, she and her son could have been dead. God knows just the right day, for a blessing too early could very well turn into a curse. God's timing is perfect.

GOD IS GOD and We are NOT!

But seek first His kingdom and His righteousness and ALL these things shall be added to you. (Matthew 6:33)

He's the Potter and we are the clay. **GOD IS GOD and We are NOT** - and He's not taking applications for His position.

St. Anthony may have said it best:

"Everyone longs to give themselves completely to someone—to have a deep soul relationship with another, to be loved thoroughly and exclusively. But God, to a Christian says, "No, not until you are satisfied with living loved by Me alone and have an intensely personal unique relationship with Me alone. I love you My child and until you discover that only in Me is your satisfaction, you will not be capable of the perfect human relationship that I have planned for you. I want you to stop planning, stop wanting and allow Me to give you the most thrilling plan existing - one that you cannot imagine. I want you to have the best. Please allow Me to bring it to you - just keep watching Me, expecting the greatest things - keep experiencing that satisfaction of knowing that I AM - keep learning and listening to the things I tell you.
You must wait. Don't be anxious. Don't worry. Don't look around at the things others have gotten or that I have given them. Don't look at the things you want. Just keep looking to Me or you will miss what I want to show you. And then, when you are ready, I will surprise you with a love far more wonderful than any you would ever dream of. You see, until you are ready and even this minute, to have both of you ready at the same time - until you are both satisfied with Me and the life I prepared for you, you won't be able to experience the love that exemplifies your relationship with Me and is thus, perfect love.
And dear one, I want you to have this most wonderful love. I want you to see in the flesh, a picture of your relationship with Me and to enjoy the everlasting union of beauty and love. I AM GOD. Believe and be satisfied.'"

1247 A. D.

The Walking of It

Dear Reader,

Please accompany me on my journey that began one memorable day in July. There I was, minding my own business, going to church. My daughter was out of town, so for the first time, I went alone. I'd been single a number of years and was silently looking forward to August, when Mikala, my youngest, would begin college, and for the first time in my life, I'd be FREE. However, God, in His magnificent wisdom, had other plans.

I repeat...there I was, minding my own business, arriving late to church, I found a seat; two seats down from a man. (A respectable distance, don't you think?)

During the meet and greet time, he said, "Hi."

I said, "Hi." (Uneventful, or so I thought.) Well, God started talking, "Barbara, that's your husband."

"No, Lord, it couldn't be, don't You see, those are POLYESTER pants he's wearing?" (I was sure that MY husband would come in silk, wool, or linen.)

God continued, "Barbara, that's your husband."

"Lord, it couldn't be. Don't You see those are COWBOY BOOTS he's wearing?" (Again, I was sure of the fact that MY husband would come in Gucci's.)

During this silent discourse with the Lord, I did however notice one thing; this man had the aura of Jesus all around him. He was oblivious to everything, but praising his God. (Too loudly, I thought; he just didn't know how sophisticated we were at that church.) So, with the utmost intent, I put these conversations aside, and TRIED to enter into the worship service. During the altar call, I went up to minister to some of the women, and cried as I prayed with them. As I was walking back to my seat at the close of the service, this man came up. I made some comment about my tears, to which he added, "Isn't it good to be able to share the pain of another person and to pray them through into healing?"

As we spoke, he invited me to lunch. What a shock. I'd always tried to keep a safe distance from guys...I'd learned a lot from a disastrous relationship. When someone would try to fix me up, I'd simply say, "No thanks, when I'm ready and he's ready, God will send him and he'll have, "From Your Father, GOD" on his forehead and I'll KNOW who he is." It seems I was grossly failing my discernment test.

My answer to his question about lunch was, "No thanks, my little girl has been out of town and I need to spend the day with her."

At this, my "little" eighteen-year-old came up, after returning from a weekend trip with the youth. She was shocked to find her mother talking to a guy. The man asked for my phone number and gave me his business card with a parting, "Give me a call." What audacity. Just WHO did he think he was? Besides, nice girls don't call guys. At that, I dismissed the whole issue with a laugh. However, the next day, the Fourth of July, he called.

"WHAT is your name?" I asked.

"Nick," he said, again.

"I'm sorry, I don't know anyone named Nick," I replied.

He proceeded to remind me of our meeting just yesterday, along with, "I wondered if you had plans for today?"

"Yes, as a matter of fact, the kid's and I are going to Memphis to shop." Now, wouldn't you think this would end the conversation? Certainly not - *The righteous are bold as a lion and the wicked flee, when no one's pursuing them (Proverbs 28:1).*

"Would you call if you get back in time to go to Pop's on the River, tonight?"

To which I replied, "I'm SURE we'll get back too late."

At that, he asked what I was doing the next day?

"I need to go to the store," I replied.

"What store?" He asked.

"My store, Barbara's Locker Room," I replied.

He continued, "Where is it? I could meet you there and take you to lunch."

I realized this guy wasn't going to go away, so I gave him directions and planned to meet him for lunch. Little did I know that he was on assignment from God and did not tell his Father, "NO."

The next day, I ran into the store, threw my briefcase over the counter, told my employees that I'd be back, and went next door to the restaurant to meet Nick for lunch. It was the MOST unusual lunch ever - ALL this man talked about was GOD. However, he was so anointed that it was OK, I didn't want to leave. Finally, after our three-hour lunch, he left. I went back to the store and tried to totally discount the whole adventure to my employees, who knew that I didn't do lunches with guys.

Later that day, I received a beautiful floral arrangement, with a card that said:

> "Many daughters have done nobly, but you excel them all." Charm is deceitful and beauty is vain, but a woman who fears the Lord, she shall be praised. (Proverbs 31:29-30)

I thought, "Oh, that's sweet." Nick later shared that it was in sheer obedience to the voice of his Father and a giant step of faith to write that scripture, as ONLY through the Spirit could he ever see those attributes coming into manifestation in the natural. You see I was an over-achieving feminist who didn't want to be bothered. Besides, what could a guy give me that I couldn't give myself? The answer? The biggest, most phenomenal God that I NEVER knew existed.

When I called Nick to thank him for the flowers he asked if he could see me again on Thursday night. He was busy ministering with an evangelist at tent revivals on Wednesday and Friday.

I said, "Yes, would you like to just come over here? We could go for a walk, or if you'd like, I have a pool, you could swim."

Thursday night arrived and I was excited. I didn't remember much about him, except the Jesus he carried. Nick came to the door wearing the most awful Pepto-Bismol pink colored dress shirt with RED RUNNING SHORTS - you know, that old-fashioned kind with a white stripe - and I OWNED a sports apparel shop. What a horribly distasteful outfit, and I'd agreed to go for a walk with him in MY neighborhood where people knew me. Oh, God! Well, thank the Lord for those times that He in His mercy and grace pushes us through our tests that we would NEVER otherwise pass.

As we started our walk I noticed his car; it was by far the shabbiest that I'd ever seen and it was parked in MY driveway on the cul-de-sac in Lakewood. I cried, "Oh, Jesus, PLEASE HELP ME. I know this is You, and I know there's nothing in me capable of passing this test."

We went for a walk, then came back to the house. I felt much more comfortable not being on parade. God showed up and anointed the time with His presence and power, beginning my death to the things of the flesh in favor of the voyage to go onward and upward with the Spirit of the Living God.

As we were sitting out by the pool, talking of heavenly things, Nick pulled out a ring from his pocket, FOR ME. OH LORD! He asked me to marry him. Seems the Lord had told him months earlier that He was sending his wife, and the size ring she wore. At this point in my life, I must admit, I'd been heavily into DIAMONDS...REAL ONES of course. With one look, I knew this ring was Cubic Zirconium. Oh, were these flesh tests ever going to cease? However, I KNEW THIS WAS GOD. In a moment's time, God overruled my brain and the word "Yes" came out of my mouth. It's so true that the flesh rails against the spirit of the Living God.

A few days later when I told my family, they were ready to have me committed. They replied as one, "You just don't do things like this; we don't even know him and neither do you." All I knew was that if I'd ever heard or seen God in my life, this was the time. In myself, I had no idea how I was going to get through this. The battle was raging between my head, my flesh, what people thought, and the spirit of the LIVING GOD.

My heavenly Father knew just what the biggest tests would be, and He was sending them all through Nick. God bless the man; he did a great job keeping his eyes on Jesus, *the author and finisher of our faith (Hebrews 12:2)* in spite of ME.

The Lord also told Nick where his future wife went to church and where to sit when he visited that church. He heard God so clearly. I found out later it was because THAT was the only voice he wanted to hear. God had taken him through his breaking from the things of this world. You see he'd also had a nice house, with a pool and all the trappings of wealth, until the hammer of God came down on his life with its sin and addictions. One night, in the midst of his breaking, he'd tried to end it all but found that God wasn't even going to let him pull that off. Instead, he just happened to turn the TV to a Christian station, by mistake, and got saved. Then, after he'd lived through his breaking, God sent him to me to guide me through mine, assuring me all the while that I WOULD live through it.

On Sunday morning, July 10, Nick was meeting me for church. I couldn't even remember what he looked like except that he wore glasses and what I considered terribly outdated clothes. As Mikala and I were walking down the hall she said, "Mom, there he is."

"Oh God." He was wearing a flowered, Hawaiian-style polyester shirt to go with his polyester pants.

"Oh, Lord, You know this is MY church where everyone likes me and not only am I going in with this guy, but I also have this imitation ring on my finger." My life, as I knew it, had come to an end in just one week. Was I going to live through it? Only GOD knew for SURE. I was beginning to realize that this man, sent from God, fit NOWHERE in my present life. However the plan of God has to go on, doesn't it?

We filed into church. I tried to praise God and discount the fact that I was sure the spotlight was shining on this most outrageous turn of events, that no one EXCEPT God and the angels were cheering on. During the worship time, as I was trying to hide the ring and act like he was some stray I'd picked up doing my good deeds, Nick bowed on his knees in prayer to his Father; praying out LOUD in the Spirit. I was mortified. He didn't know or seem to care that we were dignified at this church. All he knew was to enter into the presence of God, and by doing so expose the hearts of all those around him.

After church I told Nick I had to go home. Actually, I wanted to run so far from where I was, or just wake up and find that it had all been a bad dream. Not a chance. God was in charge and I was being burned up - my flesh, that is. My spirit, on the other hand, was fighting to live. After lunch I told Mikala, "There is NO WAY I can go through with this."

She, in her child-like faith and simplicity, answered, "Well, Mom, you know it's just your flesh that doesn't like it; and that's

only because you care so much about what people think. You know that it's God, don't you?"
"Mikala, I just can't go through with this."
I called Nick and told him that I'd made a terrible mistake. I asked him to please forgive me and suggested that maybe we could talk about everything when I got back from Hawaii. The children and I were leaving on Thursday for a ten-day vacation.
I later found out that Nick fell on the "Rock of Christ," crying out to the Father who had signed him up for this mission. God simply asked him one question, "Who brought you here?"
"You did, Lord," he answered.
"Well then, trust Me to do what I said I would do."
Needless to say God was turning up the heat in me so I HAD to see him just ONCE more. I called to see if he would like a rug I was getting rid of. If so I could bring it to his place on Wednesday night after church.
Ever the gentleman Nick said, "Sure," and gave me directions to his house.
I hit my knees, like never before, crying out to the Father, "Oh God, if this is You, PLEASE, in Your mercy, give me a desire for this man. Do whatever it takes to let me know undeniably that this is YOU."
When I arrived at his house trailer I found it immaculate and HOLY. Nick invited me in, we talked – and hugged - and I knew this was IT. I put the ring back on and told him I knew this was God but we'd just have to talk about the timing of it all when I got back from my trip.
When the children and I arrived in Hawaii, GOD really turned up the heat. The phone bill was $800.00 for ten days. The Lord truly gave me a desire for the God in this man. God had me all to Himself and talked to me like I'd never heard the voice of my Father before.
The children and I were to arrive back in Arkansas on Sunday, July 24, and the wedding was planned for the next Sunday. During the week before the wedding, I bought Nick a new wardrobe of both casual and dressy clothes. I also brought him athletic apparel from my store; sharp and MATCHING outfits complete with Reeboks, etc.
Thank you, Jesus, for Your mercy to ME. Nick was a handsome man and now that he had acceptable clothing, things

The Walking of It

were going better - except for the fact that only through God's eyes would you know that this marriage was right - I was getting a lot of flack for this move. However the Lord was clearly guiding each step to confirm that it was undeniably Him.

An interesting side note concerning all this is that two days before Nick came into my life I had gone to a Christian concert. The Lord had given me a word to share with the singer. However, since I was a woman and the singer a man, the pastor in charge would not allow it. I walked away and cried out to God for the first time, "Oh God, please send someone for me to minister with so we can deal rightly with the girls and the guys." The Lord was faithful to answer that prayer because by then it was purely for His honor and glory.

The day before the wedding, I went over to help move Nick's things to my house. I thought we'd just give all his clothes to Goodwill rather than go to the trouble of moving them because I knew he would NEVER wear them again. He got tears in his eyes, which I thought was rather strange since he'd just gotten a complete NEW wardrobe.

He later told me the story of why that incident had broken his heart. It seems that he'd been through a monumental breaking of EVERYTHING in his life: the people, places, and things. He'd been without a job for months, but God had delivered food to him on his steps and he'd always had a few dollars during that time. God had set Nick apart for Himself to burn out all the old, purify him and make him like Jesus. And God had accomplished His goal. I'd never met a man with such kindness, such meekness, and such strength. He walked as his Savior...loving, giving, thinking the best of, AND letting his God go before him. He'd been in the presence of God and it penetrated those he came in contact with. Everyone he met was forced to make a decision. Either you loved him, or you wanted to throw stones at him to get rid of the conviction power flowing through him.

Back to the clothes story. After months of being shut in with God, the Lord had given Nick a job. He was SO grateful. Each payday, after his tithes and offerings, he allocated $2.00 for new clothes. His big treat was going to The Salvation Army store to buy something. What broke his heart when I wanted to trash all his clothes, was that they were from his Father.

"I'd bought myself lots of nice things before, but those were clothes my Father bought, and they were very special to me," he said. He never told me that to make me feel bad, but only to, after the fact, fill in the pieces so I'd understand what had happened that day.

To the eye of the flesh one might think Nick had just inherited a gold mine. To the spirit, however, marrying me was the hardest test for him, because that move of obedience to the Father cost Nick his sanctuary with God - to enter into a materialistic shrine of idolatry. Yes, a beautiful home on the lake, with pool and spa, complete with all the creature comforts, sports cars, and anything money could buy. But he also was to face the biggest giants of his life. For although my children and I went to church, paid our tithes, prayed, and read the Bible, we were bowing to the *"lusts of the flesh, lusts of the eye, and the boastful pride of life" (1 John 2:15-17),* rather than bowing to the Spirit of the Living God.

It was truly the battle of David and Goliath *(1 Samuel 17).* However, over the months, we changed; never by Nick's insistence, but by his prayers. One day, as I realized how much I was changing, I blurted out, "What are you doing?"

Nick answered meekly, "Barbara, I'm just praying for God to change me to love you like you need to be loved."

As a convert, I can tell you, God answers prayers like that. Since that time, as Mikala and I deal with different issues, she's quick to comment, "Mom, remember how dad came into our lives, and we changed by his example. He never laid down the law to us or tried to straighten us out by demeaning us, nor did he use any negative words. But by his prayers, love, and compassion - always uplifting and encouraging us - we DID change."

During this time, I'm sure also due to Nick's prayers and the plan of God, we were being delivered of materialism. I'd been into designer EVERYTHING. The children had the cars of their choice before their sixteenth birthdays, went to private schools, and were also into designer and snooty everything. However, God was delivering us all from our idols.

One day, Nick suggested that I read *Ezekiel 16.* After scanning it, I fumed, "I don't know who that's for. It certainly

The Walking of It

meant nothing to me." It's about the unfaithfulness of _____ - God's kids. The passage ends with:

> "Nevertheless, I will remember My covenant with you in the days of your youth, and I will establish an everlasting covenant with you. . . .and you shall know that I am the LORD, in order that you may remember and be ashamed, and never open your mouth anymore because of your humiliation, when I have forgiven you for all that you have done," declares the Lord. (Ezekiel 16:60-63)

Despite the torment Nick went through in this assignment from his Father, he prayerfully maintained the balance of loving God and the God in us, more than pleasing our flesh. Many times he wept as he sought God's heart for us. He felt the awesome responsibility of loving and gently guiding us into the ways of God, truth and LIFE. On the day of our wedding Nick told the children, "From this day forward I stand accountable at the throne of God on your behalf." He took his headship of the family as his utmost responsibility before God, knowing that someday he would give an account.

The Lord had Nick deal with me concerning pride, arrogance and haughtiness. I really didn't understand what he was talking about, so GOD came in to help with some examples. One Sunday, at church, during the ministry time, the Lord had broken my heart for all the hurting people. I cried and had mascara all over my face, THEN, the Lord gave me a Word to minister to the congregation. As I went forward to give it, my bra strap fell down (exposed before God and man) and my face was a mess. When I got to the microphone, it didn't work. God said, "Barbara, this is about the pride issue that Nick has been trying to deal with - NOW, I've taken you on."

Oh, Lord. It seemed that so many times Nick and God were playing tennis and I was the ball. I praise God that neither gave up on me.

In the past, Mikala and I had enjoyed going to the Apparel Market in Dallas, and would haul home bags of samples for ourselves. However, before the upcoming market, the Lord had been breaking me and delivering me of idolatry. As we arrived at Market, the atmosphere was terrible. It seemed we'd been transported to a hell where everyone was concerned about sizes, colors, styles, prices, etc. The GAMES PEOPLE PLAY seemed to be on a giant video screen for us to see everywhere we turned. It was disgusting. You see, God had taken me into a world where people had been coming into the store crippled and they walked out healed. They came in as sinners and walked out saved. They came in dying and left full of life. "Oh, God, that's the real stuff, isn't it?"

I called Nick and said, "This is hell and we're coming home."

So we did. Once the Lord delivered me from the materialistic games people play, then my prayer became, "Oh, God, set me free from this business that I've set up as an idol. I repent and ask you to forgive me and deliver me from this place. I just want to be free to GO…DO THE STUFF.

What stuff you ask? The stuff Jesus told His disciples to do in *Matthew 10…"Go preach the kingdom of heaven is at hand, heal the sick, raise the dead, cast out demons and set the captives free."* Read it, it's your call also.

Well, I hadn't gotten into that mess overnight - *the lust of the flesh, the lust of the eye and the boastful pride of life (1John 2:16)* - and I wasn't going to get out overnight. God wanted to be real sure I'd NEVER again walk the walk of *2 Peter 2:18-22:*

> *For speaking out arrogant words of vanity they entice by fleshly desires, by sensuality, those who barely escape from the ones who live in error, promising them freedom while they themselves are slaves of corruption; for by what a man is overcome, by this he is enslaved.*
>
> *For if after they have escaped the defilements of the world by the knowledge of the Lord and Savior Jesus Christ, they are again entangled in them and are overcome, the last state has become worse for them than the first. For it would be better for them not to have known the way of righteousness, than having known it, to turn away from the holy commandment delivered to them. It has happened to them according to the true proverb, "A dog returns to its own vomit," and "a sow, after washing, returns to wallowing in the mire."*

The Walking of It

For months, I cried out to God to set me free to *"owe no man anything but the love of Jesus Christ."* It seemed the heavens were as brass; I couldn't get through.

"Nick, what can I do to get God to answer me and set me free?"

"Barbara, ALL you have to do is praise God in EVERYTHING and do whatever He tells you, because when you praise God in everything, the devil will quit messing with you. He'll get tired of you praising God. When you decide to praise and obey God in EVERYTHING...He'll be free to move."

When Jesus was being harassed, *He said, "Begone, Satan. For it is written, 'You shall worship the Lord your God, and serve Him only.' " Then the devil left Him and behold, angels came and began to minister to Him (Matthew 4:10-11).*

I told Nick, "I'm doing EVERTYHING I know to do."

I tried and I tried, and finally, one day, I fell on the Rock *(Luke 20:18)* crying out to God, "God whatever it takes to go free, just tell me and I'll do it...I WANT TO GO...DO THE STUFF."

God said, "Go."

"But, God, You gave me this big house on the lake, with the pool and spa; everything money could buy."

"Barbara, didn't the rich young ruler say something just like that, and he could have been MY disciple?" *(See Luke 18:18-30.)*

No man can be My disciple, unless he leave it all and follow Me (Luke 14:33).

Needless to say the house went on the market and the door was locked on the store. How simple, yet how complex. Especially when you're trying to hold on to what people think, their respect, and the fear of man rather than the fear of God. *(See John 12:42-43, Galatians 1:10 and Job 32:21-22.)*

"Oh God, help me die to live." *(See John 12:24-25.)*

Then the walk of *Hebrews 11* began:

Now faith is the assurance of things hoped for, the conviction of things not seen. For by it the men of old gained approval. By faith Abel. . . . By faith Enoch was taken up so that he should not see death; and he was not found because God took him up; for he obtained the witness that before his being taken up he was pleasing to God. And without faith it is impossible to please Him, for he who comes to God must believe that He is, and that He is a rewarder of those who seek Him. By faith Noah. . . . By faith Abraham, when he was called, obeyed by going out to a place which he was to receive for an inheritance; and he went out, not knowing where he was going. By faith he lived as an alien in the land of promise, . . . for he was looking for the city which has foundations, whose architect and builder is God.

And indeed if they had been thinking of that country from which they went out, they would have had opportunity to return. But as it is, they desire a better country, that is a heavenly one. Therefore God is not ashamed to be called their God; for He has prepared a city for them.

And all these, having gained approval through their faith, did not receive what was promised, because God had provided something better for us, so that apart from us they should not be made perfect. (Hebrews 11:1-10,15-16, 39-40)

A True LOVE STORY

A letter from Nick to my daughter

Mikala:

I wanted to buy you the most precious gift for your eighteenth birthday, so I labored in prayer before God to find the one thing that would fit. What I found - I couldn't buy, but I can share it with you. As I write this, I hope you will hear the voice of God Almighty, and know that He has been with you all along.

There are very few times in our lives when we can really open our hearts up to another; so many hurts along life's path cause us to become callous, and even fearful of love. I have been a victim of this, but, when I think of the joy that you have brought into my heart - to see a smile that melts away all fears, and to watch as you grow closer to God, looking to me for wisdom. The awesomeness of God's plan overwhelms me.

I've done nothing to deserve your love but love isn't deserving. It must always be given freely, as a matter of choice, or it's not love at all but a shabby imitation, built upon self-needs.

Mikala, I love you just as you are. I wish I had been your paternal father; to have given you my life, to watch your birth, hear you cry, to send you off to kindergarten, then on to high school. To watch you grow each day, feeding you of God's word, knowing that some day I would have to let you go for another man. I know that even now as you prepare for him and the life to come many changes will take place in you, for you are a woman, not a child any longer.

You have put away the things of this life and have chosen to follow the path laid out before you; following a man from Galilee, bare-footed and meek in appearance. God has blessed you with beauty beyond compare and a mind that is quick and sharp. I am blessed to know you. I am truly blessed to call you my daughter - and you are - for we are together. I thank you for being my friend, and for allowing me to be a part of your life that will remain forever.

Two things I've found to be true:
1. Wait upon the Lord, and when He speaks, obey. Whatever it is, do it; don't rely on your own knowledge or understanding *(Psalm 37:4-7)*.
2. Trust God.
Trust in the Lord, and do good. . . Delight yourself in the Lord; and He will give you the desires of your heart. Commit your way to the Lord, trust also in Him, and He will do it. And He will bring forth your righteousness as the light, and your judgment as the noonday. Rest in the Lord and wait patiently for Him. (Psalm 37:3-7)

You will constantly find yourself living in these places:
And without faith; it is impossible to please Him, for he who comes to God must believe that He is, and that He is a rewarder of those who seek him. By faith Noah, being warned by God about things not yet seen, in reverence prepared an ark for the salvation of his household, by which he condemned the world, and became an heir of the righteousness which is according to faith. By faith, Abraham, when he was called, obeyed by going out to a place which he was to receive for an inheritance; and he went out, not knowing where he was going. (Hebrews 11:6-8)

Prompted by faith, urged on by faith. Remember, that what you can see isn't real, but what you can't see "the Spirit realm," that is real *(Romans 8:24-25)*. God is not seen, but He is eternal. I don't know of anything that will stop you quicker than family or friends. They will say, "You can't do that," or "You have gone too far." Well, you haven't, keep going. You have a long way to go - so - GO on.

Let no one keep you from the Truth. JESUS is the Truth. The Holy Spirit leads us to Jesus. It's His job to show us the things that belong to Christ.

But I tell you the truth, it is to your advantage that I go away; for if I do not go away, the Helper shall not come to you; but if I go, I will send Him to you. And He, when He comes, will convict the world concerning sin, righteousness and judgment; concerning sin, because they do not believe in Me; and concerning righteousness, because I go to the Father, and you no longer behold Me; and concerning judgment, because the ruler of this world has been judged.

I have many more things to say to you, but you cannot bear them now. But when He, the Spirit of truth comes, He will guide you into all the truth; for He will not speak on His own initiative, but whatever He hears, He will speak; and He will disclose to you what is to come. He shall glorify Me; for He shall take of Mine, and shall disclose it to you. All things that the Father has are Mine; therefore I said, that He takes of Mine, and will disclose it to you. (John 16:7-15)

Don't let the doubt and disbelief of others get in your way. You ARE going somewhere. Doubt and disbelief will destroy dreams and desires; they will kill you spiritually. Don't let that happen.

You and your husband won't get together by looking for each other. God has it all planned. You simply walk it out. Don't try it another way, just keep a firm hold on the Word of God and continually surrender yourself to the cross. Kill the flesh and its desires, so that God can use you. He won't use flesh; it must die. You are God's sheep, not gods. HE is your provider, healer, helper, lover, and friend; whatever He needs to be, He is.

And God said to Moses, "I AM WHO I AM;" and He said, "Thus you shall say to the sons of Israel, 'I AM has sent me to you."' (Exodus 3:14)

These things are true - faith, hope and love, yet love is the greatest. Read, study and pray *1 Corinthians 13*. Love is give, not take. Love is help, not hinder. Love thinks the best, hopes the best, wants the best for others; not for self.

Don't let people, places, or things get in the way of you doing what God has told you to do.

Praise God at ALL times, for ALL things, ALL THINGS, ALL THINGS. Whether they seem good or advantageous or if in dire straits, PRAISE GOD AND BE THANKFUL.

One thing I want to impress upon you is that God's plan is for you to die to yourself, and serve and please Him. Remember, **GOD IS GOD**, not self. WE LOVE YOU.

There is no wisdom greater than God's. God's word is a part of God, and all His words are *"alive and active and sharp as a two-edge sword"* (Hebrews 4:12).

As you walk through this life, remember: *Greater is He, who is in you than he who is in the world* (1 John 4:4).

He is sufficient...Who began such a great work in you, to bring it to fullness, complete in Christ Jesus, our blessed Messiah. I can find no greater love than that of Jesus, so I refer you to Him. He is the wisdom that is talked about in the Book of Proverbs. My daughter:

Hear your father's instruction, and do not forsake the teaching of your mother; indeed, they are a graceful wreath to your head, and ornaments about your neck. (Proverbs 1:8-9)

I find no wrong in you, a heart so pure and clean. I know you and see you as a spotless lamb before God, choose to stay that way. Choose life in Christ, no matter what the cost; choose to stay soft before Him, that He might use you to deliver His people.

THERE IS NO POWER WITHOUT PURITY, and NO PURITY WITHOUT PRAYER.

Purpose in your heart every day to find one person you can give to. Give a smile, a soft word, a cheerful greeting - give until it hurts, then, give again, until it feels good. The saying is true and bears repeating: you cannot out-give God. What you sow will be reaped, tear for tear, and joy for joy *(Galatians 6:7)*. God will not be mocked, nor made a liar. We all err, but we have a mediator to go before God for us, even Christ Jesus. *(See 1 Timothy 2:5)*

In ALL things, honor the other person above yourself; forgive quickly, repent quickly, and receive quickly.

Always forgive and never hesitate, or loathe anyone for what they have done, but thank God that you weren't put in their position.

Praise God always, no matter how you feel, even when upset by circumstances, for He gave you life. Don't let ANYTHING steal your joy. A Christian without joy is a dead duck.

Doubt, despair, and depression - destroy dreams and desires. Fear, frustration, and folly - fracture faith.

A True LOVE STORY

Two things I asked of Thee, do not refuse me before I die: keep deception and lies far from me, give me neither poverty nor riches; feed me with the food that is my portion, lest I be full and deny Thee and say, "Who is the Lord?" Or lest I be in want and steal, and profane the name of my God. (Proverbs 30:7-9)

There are three places you can go; to the books of Job, Ecclesiastes, and Psalms, to find that you are not alone. Many times I have faced fear, doubt, and even the lies of the evil one; then run to God and found Him there with my friends.

Mikala, even if Noah, Daniel, and Job were all here now, they couldn't save anyone but themselves *(Ezekiel 14:12-20)*. Even Paul, John the Baptist, and Peter could only lead others to Christ, who is our Savior. He and He alone can save souls.

You are precious in God's sight; He has named you after Himself, and He has called you His very own. What a price He did pay. He gave His only begotten Son, just for you, just as you are. This is a principle of God's - to give. God gave, knowing that only through the death of His Son could He redeem a nation of lost sheep - children that would turn their backs on Him, as quickly as they could.

God said, "Let your yes be yes, and your no, no; so that you may not fall under judgment." (James 5:12)

Thumper's mother said, "If you don't have anything nice to say, don't say anything at all."

Death and life are in the power of the tongue, and those who love it will eat its fruit. (Proverbs 18:21)

Spend time in *James 3*. Listen and learn from the mistakes of others, that you need not make them yourself.

You are a lamp set upon a hillside, that can't be hidden. You are the salt of the earth, to preserve and to irritate *(Matthew 5:13-14)*. Don't be ashamed that you're different, but rejoice that God has found you worthy to serve Him.

I've heard it said, and I agree, that experience is recognizing a mistake and not making it again.

My life has been full, but not complete. Thank you for sharing your life with me, and for helping me be the best dad I can be. Happy Birthday...I Love You...

Nick

GET YOUR HOUSE IN ORDER
A test in the sovereignty of GOD

On February 10, two and a half years into the journey with Nick, the Lord told us that we had two weeks to get our house in order. Thinking that we were returning to Israel, we gave notice to the landlord and began to prepare to leave.

February 17, at church, Brother Carl, who moved in the prophetic, said, "Nick, God has heard your prayers and you get to go back to Heaven." Nick was thrilled with this good news, as we'd both been there before, in dreams and visions, as had Paul *(2 Corinthians 12:1-4)* and John *(Revelation 4:1-2)*.

On Friday, February 22, Nick and I went into the city for a weekend seminar and checked into the Holiday Inn. On Saturday night, Nick didn't feel well, so we stayed at the hotel. As I was praying for him, the Lord gave me *Ezekiel 24:16-18*:

"Son of man, behold, I am about to take from you the desire of your eyes with a blow; but you shall not mourn, and you shall not weep, and your tears shall not come. Groan silently; make no mourning for the dead. Bind on your turban, and put your shoes on your feet, and do not cover your mustache, and do not eat the bread of men." So I spoke to the people in the morning, and in the evening, my wife died. And in the morning, I did as I was commanded.

Later that evening Nick was feeling worse. As I was praying for him the pain left him and the peace of God came into the room. I saw a vision of Nick at the throne of God.

Boasting is necessary, though it is not profitable; but I will go on to visions and revelations of the Lord. I know a man in Christ who fourteen years ago - whether in the body I do not know, or out of the body I do not know, God knows - such a man was caught up to the third heaven. And I know how such a man - whether in the body or apart from the body I do not know, God knows - was caught up into Paradise, and heard inexpressible words, which a man is not permitted to speak. (2 Corinthians 12:1-4)

Get Your House in Order

By Sunday, Nick's condition still hadn't changed but he refused to see a doctor and I respected his decision. So at checkout time, we left for home.

Nick slept until 4 a.m. Monday morning at which time he woke up and asked me to read Psalm 35 to him. Then he went back to sleep. At 1 p.m. he died.

Mikala, who had been downstairs in her room, came up and called 911. Within minutes the house was full of firefighters and paramedics. She and I were praying in the Spirit and singing, "LAZARUS, COME FORTH."

The paramedics took Nick to the hospital in the ambulance with Mikala and I following. The nurse put us in the family room where we continued singing and praising our God.

A few minutes later the nurse returned to say, "Mrs. Antuna, I'm afraid there's nothing more we can do for your husband."

I replied, "Well, he's at the throne of God now and if God plans to bring him back, He will."

She looked rather puzzled.

I tried to explain, *"The Lord gives and the Lord takes away. Blessed be the name of the Lord"* (Job 1:21b).

At that she informed me that I needed to make arrangements with a funeral home for disposal of the body following the autopsy at 9 a.m. the next morning.

I could just see Nick returning and finding himself in a morgue, so I asked what I thought was a reasonable question. "Will there be anyone in there with him tonight?"

Before we left the hospital, a detective arrived to question me about Nick's death. He asked if he could follow me home to get more information. I got to do some great (or so I thought) preaching. After three hours, he left. I packed Nick's bag with his shoes and warm-up suit and waited for the call – I expected Nick, like Lazarus, to come forth.

The next morning at 8:58, two minutes before the autopsy was scheduled to begin, God said, "Barbara, we have to talk."

"What, Lord?"

"Will you praise Me as much, if I don't raise him, as if I do?"

"Well, yes, Lord."

"Will you believe in resurrection as much, if I don't raise him as if I do?"

"Yes, Lord."

To that the Lord replied, "Nick has been here two days and he's doing everything he ever wanted to do." (You see, all Nick wanted to do was to throw his crown at his Savior's feet and praise Him forever and ever, AMEN.)

"God, bless that holy man for me," was all I could reply.

I knew then that the autopsy would begin at 9 a.m. as scheduled. An interesting side-note...when I arrived home from the Emergency Room, Nick's Bible, the one he NEVER wrote in, was turned to *Isaiah 54:4b-5,* and underlined:

And the reproach of your widowhood you will remember no more. For your husband is your Maker, whose name is the Lord of hosts; and your Redeemer is the Holy One of Israel, who is called the God of all the earth.

As Mikala and I prayed about what had just happened, the Lord gave us *Psalm 101:6...*

My eyes shall be upon the faithful of the land, that they may dwell with me; He who walks in a blameless way is the one who will minister to Me.

What a promotion!

Later that day, the Lord said we were to get Nick's things out of the house before we went to bed that night. Also, that I was to sell his Jeep. By midnight, everything was packed and labeled to be shipped to ministers who would carry the torch onward.

Early Tuesday morning, the Lord gave me my next assignment. Life goes on; each page, each chapter, written on by the hand of the Living God and with praises, we serve HIM.

Tuesday, as Mikala and I were packing to move, the detective returned. I think they must have thought I'd killed him, but God had assured me that the autopsy report would exonerate me. After seemingly hours of interrogation, God said to me, "I'm giving him three more questions, then you'll NEVER see him again." Well, hallelujah and thank You, Jesus.

The three questions began:
   1. "Did Nick have life insurance?"
      "No."

2. "Do you have a means to support yourself?"
"Yes, I have a triple Master's degree."
3. "Do you believe in doctors?"
"I suppose, IF you need them."

At that he left, never to return again. However, the Lord asked me, "Barbara, would you go to jail for Me?"

"Well, yes, Lord, I'll go anywhere You want me to go."

At that it seemed the issue was dropped, and life went on. Mikala and I moved to the apartment the Lord had given us...to begin again.

In August, however, I received notice of a Grand Jury Investigation, into the death of Nicholas Maurillio Antuna. It did mention one item, however, that I took offense with. It suggested that if I chose to come I should bring counsel. To which I replied, "Now devil, you think you're going to invite me to a party and I have to HIRE a friend to come with me? NO WAY." At that I burned the letter, so similar to the one from *Sennacherib (2 Kings 18-19).*

Later, the prosecuting attorney called to see if I would allow Mikala to testify, to which I replied, "Sure, Michael, I've got nothing to hide."

For Mikala's twenty-first birthday she got to testify before a Grand Jury Investigation into the death of her dad...God sure knows how to grow His kids up. They even paid her expenses for the day. *The wealth of the wicked is stored up for the righteous. (Proverbs 13:22b)*

You see, a day is just a day, and **GOD IS GOD** and He can sign His kid's up for whatever HE desires. It's HIS school and He knows what we need to learn for where He wants to use us.

That evening I received a call from the prosecuting attorney who informed me that I was being charged with second degree murder in Nick's death. He also shared that, normally, an officer would be sent to pick me up for the arraignment the next morning. However, he didn't feel that would be necessary because he trusted me to be there. He didn't know that my GOD had signed me up for this and I was expectantly awaiting this miraculous showdown. Hallelujah. GOD ALWAYS WINS.

The next morning I gave God my emotions and proceeded to the Courthouse with the Sword of the Lord - my Bible - at my side. As I waited the Lord allowed me to minister to several people. Soon, Michael, the prosecuting attorney, arrived. We exchanged greetings and walked into the Judge's chambers. Since I had no job at the time, the Judge appointed me a public defender. They all agreed to release me on my own recognizance and I was told to go to the jail to be fingerprinted. After receiving directions, I continued on my adventure.

Singing praises to God, I was ushered past two security doors and sent in to the jail matron, who I quickly found out was going through a nasty divorce. We had a wonderful prayer meeting, hands uplifted, praising our God; UNTIL, a Sheriff came running in thinking there was a problem. I assured him that everything was fine; we were just praising God and he was welcome to join us. At that invitation he fled from the room.

Several weeks later my court appointed attorney gave me all the testimony from the Grand Jury investigation to refute. My TOTAL defense was the WORD of GOD. Shouldn't I use the BEST defense? This was God's deal and He would be fighting the battle.

For the word of God is living and active and sharper than any two-edged sword, and piercing as far as the division of soul and spirit, of both joints and marrow, and able to judge the thoughts and intentions of the heart. (Hebrews 4:12)

The points I had to refute were:
1. "She was glad he died."
    The Word of God says in *Ephesians 5:20:*
    Always giving thanks for ALL things in the Name of our Lord Jesus Christ to God, even the Father.
    In everything give thanks; for this is God's will for you in Christ Jesus. (1 Thessalonians 5:18)
2. "She thought he would come back."
    I do believe in the resurrection of the dead, and that God is sovereign. I didn't know how God would answer.
    And when He had said these things, He cried out with a loud voice, "Lazarus, come forth." He who had died came forth, bound hand and foot with wrappings; and his face was wrapped around with a cloth. Jesus said to them, "Unbind him, and let him go." (John 11:43-44)

Get Your House in Order

And when I saw Him, I fell at His feet as a dead man. And He laid His right hand upon me, saying, "Do not be afraid; I am the first and the last, and the living One; and I was dead, and behold, I am alive forevermore, and I have the keys of death and of Hades." (Revelation 1:17-18)

3. "She was speaking in another language."
It was tongues, the heavenly language that grants you direct access to the Father.

And in the same way the Spirit also helps our weakness; for we do not know how to pray as we should, but the Spirit Himself intercedes for us with groanings too deep for words; and He who searches the hearts knows what the mind of the Spirit is, because He intercedes for the saints according to the will of God. (Romans 8:26-27)

And there appeared to them tongues as of fire distributing themselves, and they rested on each one of them, and they were ALL filled with the HOLY SPIRIT and began to speak with other tongues. (Acts 2:3-4)

So, that was my TOTAL defense...page after page of the WORD of GOD - the best defense possible. My attorney, however, grew increasingly irate with my answers to his questions. Especially, as I quoted Apostle Paul, *"I am on trial for the hope and resurrection of the dead" (Acts 23:6b).*

At that my attorney tried to reason with me. "Does your family know anything about this?"

"Well, no. There's not a problem here, why should I involve them? God said this is stupid and He's going to throw it out."

"BARBARA, YOU'RE LOOKING AT PRISON."

"If God sends me to prison, then we'll have revival there."

At that he threw the papers down on his desk and stormed out of the room. It was then I noticed a painting on his wall that I'd never seen before. It was of Martin Luther, peering over the Bible by candlelight.

The Lord said, "I've been trying for years to get this man to read My Word, and now the state is paying him to read it." God is so wise. He knows where we all live and how to take us from where we are to where He has designed us to be - one day at a time. Sweet Jesus! For you see, I at NO time had a problem. When God signs you up for something, it's ALL in HIS hands and you just walk it out. Why is it that we would consider it an honor to go to the President with a word from the Lord, but not to a jail matron, a judge, a lawyer, or to a prosecuting attorney? You see, I would just never have thought to pay any of those folks a visit that day, but that's why God is in charge of our agendas. **GOD IS GOD and We are NOT** and He can get us through any door.

He who is holy, who is true, who has the key of David, who opens and no one will shut, and who shuts and no one opens, says this: "I know your deeds. Behold, I have put before you an open door which no one can shut. . ." (Revelation 3:7)

Here are some behind the scene notes on this escapade:
1. When God asked if I'd go to jail for Him, He shared that many of His kid's wimp out when it comes to tough assignments.
2. Also, the second-degree murder charge was because I did not take Nick to the doctor. Nick DID NOT go to doctors. Nick had always said, "If the God who made me doesn't heal me - leave it alone." We'd both seen numerous miracles and experienced healing from the hand of God.
3. Nick was a big man - I didn't TAKE him anywhere.
4. During this time, the media was filled with stories of a similar case before the State Supreme Court concerning the death of a child who had not been taken to the doctor by his parents because of their religious beliefs. This made the circumstances surrounding Nick's death, without seeing a doctor, questionable to the prosecuting attorney.
5. The autopsy report said that he had died of a diabetic coma, although he'd never been sick until that weekend.

In late November the Lord told me to go back to Arkansas because my mother was sick. When I notified my attorney of this plan, he immediately responded, "The judge will never allow that."

"Well," I told him, "that's what God said, and I've already given notice at both my apartment and job."

We had a meeting with the Judge, and he, praise God for the favor of the Lord, asked if I'd come back for trial.

I replied, "Well, yes, IF there is one."

The judge granted my request and allowed me to move.

Remember, God had been saying for months that this court case was stupid, and He was going to throw it out. Brothers and sisters, whose report was I to believe? The lawyers or the Lord's? I SHALL BELIEVE THE REPORT OF THE LORD.

God sent a brother and sister to give all our stuff to, so the move was simple - just pack our bags and go.

The trial date was set for late February. My family, however, knew NOTHING about this; until my lawyer's private investigator called me at my mother's house. After answering the investigator's questions, I figured it was time to fill my mother in on some of the details. She was shocked. I just didn't come from a family that had ever been in trouble with the law.

"Mother, God said it's stupid and He's going to throw it out."

Around the middle of February the Lord said to move to California to *"live in houses we didn't build and eat food we didn't grow"* (Deuteronomy 6:10-11). The trip was to be the last of February as was the trial date. So, whose report shall we believe? The righteous are going to be found *"living by faith"* (Hebrews 10:38) and *"what is not of faith, is sin"* (Romans 14:23).

The Monday before the trial was to start, my attorney called, SHOCKED, to inform me that the Judge had thrown the whole case out, deeming it frivolous.

"That's what God's been saying the whole time," I reminded him. HALLELUJAH. It's on the road again, onward and upward, with the King of kings and the Lord of lords; where He leads, I will go. AMEN

Editorial Update

The Lord brought Nick into our lives for two and a half years to totally change us and make us useable for the Kingdom of God. On the way home from the Emergency Room, the day of his death, Mikala said, "Mom, if God would have said that you could have the VERY BEST, but you could only keep him for two and a half years, would you do it?" I would've said, "Yes!"

God used that earthen vessel named Nick to heal a little girl's heart of rejection and fears. He encouraged her to be all that God had for her to be. He was there to teach her the ways of the Lord.

The week before he went to be with the Lord, Nick told her, "Mikala, I just heard a mother whose son was killed in Desert Storm say, 'It's just OK, because we always lived loving and hugging because you never know when it will be the last time.'" He was sharing just how important that lifestyle is because you just never know when you won't be able to tell the important people in your life, "I love you," again.

Later, while testifying before the Grand Jury Investigation, concerning his death, as they were asking meticulous, non-personal questions, she began to cry. The judge called a recess for her to compose herself. Later, He asked if she was ready to continue?

Mikala answered, "My dad was a real person. Doesn't anyone care that I'd just made him his favorite; lemon meringue pie and he never got to eat it?"

A few days after Nick's home-going, Mikala said, "You know, Mom, I'm not sure I hugged dad the LAST TIME when y'all left on Friday, because I was in a hurry to go to the grocery store."

That night, Mikala had a dream in which she was sitting in the back of a big auditorium, and someone came up, and put his arm around her. She looked and it was Nick! She got her LAST HUG. She said, "But Mom, Dad's hair was partly gray."

God knows the things His children need to have settled to go forward. Line upon line, precept upon precept, perfect, from the hand of Almighty God. He, in His mercy and love, gave His little girl the completion of that chapter.

The Sovereignty of GOD

GOD IS GOD and You are NOT and I am NOT! HE alone is worthy to hold that position - and He's not taking applications for His replacement.

I am the Lord your God. . . .You shall have no other gods before Me. (Exodus 20:2-3)

And this is eternal life, that they may know Thee, the only true God, and Jesus Christ, whom Thou hast sent. (John 17:3)

Lucifer was kicked out of heaven for wanting to BE God. Adam and Eve were kicked out of the garden for the same reason. Brothers and sisters, it behooves us to know God and His ways. He makes His view really clear in *Isaiah 46:9-13:*

Remember the former things long past, for I am God, and there is no other; I am God, and there is no one like Me, declaring the end from the beginning and from ancient times things which have not been done. Saying, "My purpose will be established, and I will accomplish all My good pleasure; calling a bird of prey from the east, the man of My purpose from a far country. Truly I have spoken; truly I will bring it to pass. I have planned it, surely I will do it. Listen to Me, you stubborn-minded, who are far from righteousness. I bring near My righteousness, it is not far off; and My salvation will not delay. And I will grant salvation in Zion, and My glory for Israel."

So complex, yet so simple:

Jesus said, "Truly I say to you, unless you are converted and become like children, you shall not enter the kingdom of God." (Matthew 18:3)

How do we come as children so we'll get in? It seems we must simply walk with God, one day at a time, and learn HIS ways.

Paul said, "That I may know Him, and the power of His resurrection and the fellowship of His sufferings." (Philippians 3:10)

One summer day, at the Falls of Engedi, Israel, where David hid out from Saul, we were watching children climb the cliffs and jump off the rocks into the water. Suddenly an Arab boy, about twelve years of age, fell and DIED right in front of us. Instantly about twenty members of his family surrounded him.

My immediate response was, "Let's go pray that God will raise him from the dead." Seemed a plausible solution for a kid lying dead from a broken neck. I was sure the entire family would be saved on the spot IF God would just show up. He's done it before and He can do it again. Right?

God said, VERY STERNLY, "Don't you dare."

"How is that God? I'm just sure the whole family would get saved IF You would just raise their little boy from the dead."

Well, HE didn't and I knew from the tone of my Father's voice to leave it alone. However, it really bothered me.

"How is it, God, that You wouldn't do that? We could have had revival." It was later, at the Pool of Bethesda, *(John 5:1-17)* that He answered, "Barbara, just like it was 2,000 years ago when I told My Son to walk amongst the sick in this place and heal only one, you also listen and move only at My leading."

Truly, truly, I say to you, the Son can do nothing of Himself, unless it is something He sees the Father doing; for whatever the Father does, these things the Son also does in like manner. For the Father loves the Son, and shows Him all things that He Himself is doing; and greater works than these will He show Him, that you may marvel. (John 5:19-20)

God's always had plenty of power; so did Jesus because HE only did what His Father was doing. God is awesome and He's going to be GOD - HIS way. He can choose to heal or to let die. God has full access to our lives.

When God was preparing me to go forth, I had a vision. The Lord said, "Barbara, today I am going to teach you about LIFE." He took me to the first of three rooms. It was full of statues, life-size and real looking, BUT they were all made of wood, or so it seemed. There were toy-soldiers, parrots, palm trees, musical instruments, a merry-go-round; the room was full of wonderful things, but all were DEAD.

God said, "Barbara, there's LIFE in your hands. Go in and everything you touch, tell it to live in My name, and it will."

I went into the room and He was right. EVERYTHING I touched came to life. The birds started singing, the soldiers started marching, the merry-go-round started turning, the palm

The Sovereignty of God

trees started waving their branches, the musical instruments started playing the most beautiful songs in praises to God. It was wonderful. EVERYTHING lived and was full of life. Hallelujah, it works. JESUS gave us life to live and life to give.

The second room looked the same, however, the Lord said, "In this room only some things will live. I'll go with you and show you which ones to touch." That was okay too. I liked this **life** stuff, even though I didn't understand why I could only touch some things in this room.

In the third room the Lord admonished me sternly, "In this room some things are to live, some will die, and some you will never know." That room was SO solemn, almost spooky, but God was there – so - not to worry. However, at this room He stood at the door and I had to listen VERY carefully to hear for SURE which things to touch with LIFE, which would die, and which to leave alone. It was an awesome responsibility, but God was at the door calling the shots.

It's HIS show and we're just along for the ride. Eternity will show whether we walked with Him in obedience or rebellion. Isn't free will actually rebellion to God? The roadways are littered with people who chose free will *(James 4:4)* and *"all that is in the world, the lust of the flesh and the lust of the eyes and the boastful pride of life,"* 1 John 2:15-16, rather than the call of God on their lives. Some are called, but chose not to be chosen *(Matthew 22:14).*

Well, what about it? This is for you. This is for me. Today. We all get to choose, and one day we'll hand the book of our lives back to God. On that day we'll find it was those daily decisions that shaped our eternity. Choose to die to all that the flesh desires, to live. Today, choose to be chosen for the call that God has for your life.

Brothers and sisters, whoever or whatever is standing between you and God simply must go. Nothing is worth missing God and His call on your life. What do you have in God's most holy and jealous spot? God is calling His children today. Try inserting your name in *Isaiah 40-43, 60-62,* and *John 14-17.* It's for you; it's for me...We are who it's written to. Receive it and be blessed. Walk it and talk it.

One day God said to Jeremiah:

> *"If you return, then I will restore you - before Me you will stand; and if you extract the precious from the worthless, you will become My spokesman. They for their part may turn to you, but as for you, you must not turn to them. Then I will make you to this people a fortified wall of bronze; and though they fight against you, they will not prevail over you; for I am with you to save you and deliver you," declares the Lord. "So I will deliver you from the hand of the wicked, and I will redeem you from the grasp of the violent." (Jeremiah 15:19-21)*

Interesting how God always says, **"IF."** Jesus always said, *"IF any man will come"* (Luke 14:26-35). God won't MAKE anyone do anything. Obedience is a choice and it's always the dividing issue. One day, the Lord stands before us with the question Elijah asked on Mount Carmel in *1 Kings 18:21...*

> *How long will you hesitate between two opinions? If the Lord is God, follow Him; but if Baal, follow him.*

To choose to be chosen. Forsake it all, what people think and those things that hold us back, to follow the Galilean with nail-scarred hands. "Wherever He leads, I'll go" and "though none go with me, I'm going." Today, go onward and upward, with God pulling you up those stairs and some big angels behind you pushing. So many of the people, places, and things just can't go - they'd just hold you back. Everyone gets a life. Everyone has their own choices to make. God bless them, but one day we have to say with Joshua:

> *Now therefore, fear the Lord and serve Him in sincerity and truth; and put away the gods, which your fathers served beyond the River and in Egypt, and serve the Lord. And if it is disagreeable in your sight to serve the Lord, choose for yourselves today whom you will serve; but as for me and my house, we will serve the Lord. (Joshua 24:14-15)*

Once you make the decision to follow Jesus with everything you are, the God of the universe will move heaven, earth and hell on your behalf. I pray, *Revelation 3:7-13,* for you today:

> *He who is holy, who is true, who has the key of David, who opens and no one will shut, and who shuts and no one opens, says this: "I know your deeds. Behold, I have put before you an open door which no one can shut,*

because you have a little power, and have kept My word, and have not denied My name. Behold, I will cause those of the synagogue of Satan, who say that they are Jews, and are not, but lie—behold, I will make them to come and bow down at your feet, and to know that I have loved you.

Because you have kept the word of My perseverance, I also will keep you from the hour of testing, that hour which is about to come upon the whole world, to test those who dwell upon the earth. I am coming quickly; hold fast what you have, in order that no one take your crown. He who overcomes, I will make him a pillar in the temple of My God, and he will not go out from it anymore; and I will write upon him the name of My God, and the name of the city of My God, the new Jerusalem, which comes down out of heaven from My God, and My new name. He who has an ear, let him hear what the Spirit says to the churches."

May God open new doors of opportunity for you. I ask Him to erase that old chalkboard of your life and to give you a brand new one, written on by the very hand of God *(Daniel 5)*.

Oh Lord today, give this child of Yours a fresh vision, renew his/her purpose, rekindle hope, impart life to live and to give.

I speak life to every cell of your being today. I come against the death, discouragement, and the lies that have come against you. I command them to be gone, in JESUS mighty name. Oh, Father, nurse this child of Yours back to health, I pray. Take away the defilement and curses of the past; heal, deliver, and forgive. Lord, I pray for new beginnings, from the throne of the living God on each reader's behalf, today; fresh, full to overflowing, and free.

Every good thing bestowed and every perfect gift is from above, coming down from the Father of lights, with whom there is no variation, or shifting shadow. (James 1:17)

Help this reader to know that You in Your mercy and goodness have saved the best wine for last *(John 2)*. I speak restoration and resurrection life to this child of Yours today, in Jesus most holy and blessed name. Amen and Amen.

Live In Houses You Didn't Build

The Lord told me in early February that Mikala and I were to go to California and take only our clothes. He'd given us Deuteronomy 6:10-11:

> Then it shall come about when the Lord your God brings you into the land which He swore to your fathers, Abraham, Isaac and Jacob, to give you, great and splendid cities which you did not build, and houses full of all good things which you did not fill, and hewn cisterns which you did not dig, vineyards and olive trees which you did not plant, and you shall eat and be satisfied.

To my mother's chagrin, I loaded up the car and took her ONLY granddaughter to CALIFORNIA. I told my mom, "Mother, we'll be fine. You know God has always taken care of us."

We arrived in California one year after Nick's death. The Lord was teaching us:

> At the command of the Lord, they camped, and at the command of the Lord they set out; they kept the Lord's charge. (Numbers 9:23)

Likewise, the New Testament version:

> The wind blows where it wishes and you hear the sound of it, but do not know where it comes from and where it is going, so is everyone who is born of the Spirit. (John 3:8)

We arrived at the San Clemente Holiday Inn, where we were going to stay, until further notice. It was a lovely place and if I'd had more faith, I would have enjoyed it much more. However, we were running out of money. Toward the end of the second week we were getting ready to sleep on the beach, so it sounded like a great time to fast and pray. Praise God that He hears and answers the cries of His children; that His sheep do hear their Father's voice. The Lord instructed us to go to the Senior Citizen's Shared Housing Program. I did, asking for our home. The director, while trying to sort all this out, said, "Well, I do have an eighty-year-old blind man whose wife is dying and he desperately needs help caring for her."

Live in Houses You Didn't Build

Sounded like God to me. He makes people so desperate; they will go against their logic and head to have their needs met.

At that, she called the man, who agreed to interview us for the position. When we arrived I said, "God, she looks dead, and this whole place feels dead."

"Well, let's raise the dead then!" was His reply.

Dr. B. seemed delighted that he got TWO for the price of one. He did, however, make one resolute condition, "I don't want you to preach to me about religion because I decided fifty years ago that if my wife could go against her entire Sicilian Catholic family to marry a blind man, the least I could do was become a Catholic for her."

Oh well, the good doctor was soon to learn that God has a tendency to break out when you least expect Him. It's very hard, even impossible, to contain the God of the Universe, especially when He's given His children the charge that He gave to Joshua, *"Every place on which the sole of your foot treads, I have given it to you, just as I spoke to Moses" (Joshua 1:3).*

We moved into our new home overlooking the ocean with room, board, and a salary. We traded in our home on the lake for one overlooking the ocean, with all expenses paid. HALLELUJAH. God is so good. Praise His holy and blessed Name, for He only is worthy of ALL praise and adoration.

In June, after several months of prayer and nursing, Mrs. B. died. Sometime later, the Lord had me share with Dr. B., "You will not go to a nursing home, and you will not linger or suffer, but when you're ready, God will come to get you." That made him cry, for only God knew those were his greatest fears.

Whenever I'd go out I'd always ask if there was anything he needed. One day in August he said, "Yes, I'd like you to get me the Chronological Bible you were talking about." Hallelujah, IT WORKS. God comes where He calls us to serve.

I told him I had one and asked if he'd like me to start reading it to him in the mornings after breakfast.

His response, "Yes, I'd like that, thank you."

The next morning our Bible study began. As we started in Matthew he commented, "I remember that from when I was a child and went to Sunday School with the neighbors." God was opening up whole new realms for that blind man. I'd wanted his eyes to open, but God instead opened his spirit eyes to see God and learn His ways…to bring life and salvation, to calm his fears and comfort him in the loss of his wife, to teach him of HIS ways and to prepare him to meet his God.

We'd moved into their home in March. The doctor was born again *(John 3:1-21)* in August, and started loving God, desiring to know His ways. The Lord used the story of Lazarus to teach Dr. B. about stewardship:

Now there was a certain rich man, and he habitually dressed in purple and fine linen, gaily living in splendor every day. And a certain poor man named Lazarus was laid at his gate, covered with sores, and longing to be fed with the crumbs which were falling from the rich man's table; besides, even the dogs were coming and licking his sores. Now it came about that the poor man died and he was carried away by the angels to Abraham's bosom; and the rich man also died and was buried.

And in Hades he lifted up his eyes, being in torment, and saw Abraham far away, and Lazarus in his bosom. And he cried out and said, "Father Abraham, have mercy on me, and send Lazarus, that he may dip the tip of his finger in water and cool off my tongue; for I am in agony in this flame." But Abraham said, "Child, remember that during your life you received your good things, and likewise Lazarus bad things; but now he is being comforted here, and you are in agony. And besides all this, between us and you there is a great chasm fixed, in order that those who wish to come over from here to you may not be able, and that none may cross over from there to us."

And he said, "Then I beg you, Father, that you send him to my father's house--for I have five brothers--that he may warn them, lest they also come to this place of torment." But Abraham said, "They have Moses and the Prophets; let them hear them."

But he said, "No, Father Abraham, but if someone goes to them from the dead, they will repent." But he said to him, "If they do not listen to Moses and the Prophets, neither will they be persuaded if someone rises from the dead." (Luke 16:19-31)

Live in Houses You Didn't Build   45

As I prayed, I kept seeing Dr. B's wife at the throne of God with NO reward. It seemed that except for a one-time building fund donation, their offering to the church had always been $1.00 each week. So, it was time to *"know the truth and the truth shall set you free," John 8:31-32.*

I continued reading the Bible to him, sharing about God's lordship over every area of our lives, including finances. I told him that one day we would each give an account before the Lord.

It is appointed for men to die once and after this comes judgment. (Hebrews 9:27)

No one can serve two masters; for either he will hate the one and love the other, or he will hold to one and despise the other. You cannot serve God and mammon (riches). (Matthew 6:24)

One day, the Lord had me share with Dr. B. that before the end of October he'd meet Jesus. I also suggested that if there was anything he'd like to do first, I'd help him. He said he'd like to go to Desert Palm Springs and visit his old home place.

He also decided to go to his doctor for a physical. Now this man seemed very healthy; he walked two miles every day, climbed mountains, and worked around the house. However, he seemed lost without his wife, so God in His mercy was preparing their re-union.

After all the tests were completed, the doctor told Dr. B. that he'd found cancer in his liver. As he was giving the prognosis, the doctor suggested that he get his house in order while he still felt like doing it.

In September, as he was finalizing the paperwork for his trust, the Lord had me share with Dr. B. that the tithe of a million-dollar estate is $100,000. He tried to convince me that surely the Lord would take the $300,000 trust that he had left to his favorite charity for the blind as settlement.

"No, Dr., actually the tithe has to be dedicated to God, for His purposes, not for yours." Thank God for HIS love and presence.

Every Sunday morning, as Dr. B. left for mass, he pulled out the first bill in his wallet, which was always $1.00 because his money was kept in numerical sequence. I knew that we had spent his last one-dollar bill on Saturday at the grocery store, and that God was dealing with him on the money issue. As he was leaving, he pulled his first bill out and asked as always, "Is this a dollar?"

I folded his wallet up, and handed it back to him with the words, "No, actually it's a $5.00 bill, but I'm sure God will find a use for it." I persevered in this matter because I knew that soon he was to meet God and I would be held accountable if I knew the truth and didn't share it.

Son of man, I have appointed you a watchman to the house of Israel; whenever you hear a word from My mouth, warn them from Me. When I say to the wicked, "You shall surely die;" and you do not warn him or speak out to warn the wicked from his wicked way that he may live, that wicked man shall die in his iniquity, but his blood I will require at your hand. Yet if you have warned the wicked, and he does not turn from his wickedness or from his wicked way, he shall die in his iniquity; but you have delivered yourself. Again, when a righteous man turns away from his righteousness and commits iniquity, and I place an obstacle before him, he shall die; since you have not warned him, he shall die in his sin, and his righteous deeds which he has done shall not be remembered; but his blood I will require at your hand. However, if you have warned the righteous man that the righteous should not sin, and he does not sin, he shall surely live because he took warning; and you have delivered yourself. (Ezekiel 3:17-21)

When Dr. B. came back from mass he shared, "Barbara, you won't believe what the Priest spoke about."

"What, Dr. B.?"

"He spoke on Lazarus and the rich man."

Praise God for backup. He never sends you anywhere in His name without backing you up. The Lord was turning up the heat and the conviction power of the Holy Spirit. The next morning he came down for breakfast and said, "I want to give $50,000 to the Lord." I must admit, the legalist in me wanted to hassle over the obvious $50,000 shortage, but God assured me that I was seeing a miracle take place before my very eyes. I asked him where he wanted it to go since he'd asked me to type the donation list.

Live in Houses You Didn't Build

Dr. B. shared that he had been especially touched by three ministries. One church he knew needed a van. The second, was a church that had been reaching out to young people and the less fortunate, making tremendous inroads for salvation and restored lives. The third was a ministry in New York City that meets the needs of the homeless, addicts, and gangs; those segments that society has given up on - unto salvation.

He started his list:
$25,000 for a new church van,
$15,000 for the gang and youth ministry, and
$10,000 to the ministry in New York City.

Now this was a MAJOR miracle. I prayed and asked God to bless his last days as I knew that after our visit to his attorney, with this last act of obedience, his house would be in order.

The morning of October 22, Dr. B. came down and said, "Let's go to Desert Palm Springs today." So, we did.

We arrived back home at dusk after climbing mountains and walking for miles. Not certain that he'd gotten in his two miles that day, Dr. B. went for another walk, listened to the World Series, then said good-night and went to his room.

The next morning, October 23, he didn't come down for breakfast. Now we always had breakfast at 7:00 EVERY morning. But this morning God said, "He won't be down, he's **in process**." Dr. B. wore an alarm around his neck for emergency situations. He never set it off that morning, and NO ONE entered his suite unless he sounded the alarm.

How is it, that even though God tells us what He is going to do, when He does it we're still shocked? God had put this little family together and now, one by one, they were going home.

At 12:43 p.m. the Lord said, "He's with Me. Call the Funeral Home."

So ended another chapter of being about the Father's business and doing what He'd called me there to do.

Because of the fear that his blindness was inherited the B's never had children. They'd devoted their lives to teaching and helping blind children. Then, in their last days, God sent them children to minister them homeward, to their reward with love. We were to do for them as unto the Lord, knowing that one-day we would give account for how we had stewarded that responsibility. Hallelujah. God rules and He reigns. And one day we shall meet again.

During our eighteen month California vacation we lived rent free in three wonderful homes, the last an estate in the midst of avocado and orange orchards, complete with a beautifully landscaped pool, spa, waterfall, cliff diving site, lots of palm trees AND a gardener. God just kept out-doing Himself, proving daily, beyond a shadow of doubt, Jesus' words:

> *Truly I say to you, there is no one who has left house or wife or brothers or parents or children, for the sake of the kingdom of God, who shall not receive many times as much at this time and in the age to come, eternal life.*
> (Luke 18:29-30)

However, one word of warning to the discerning reader, the FIRST word was, *"Sell it all and follow ME"* backed by the scriptural admonition in *Luke 14:33:*

> *So therefore, no one of you can be My disciple who does not give up all his own possessions.*

God continually proved His faithfulness.

> *That the man of God may be adequate, equipped for every good work. (2 Timothy 3:17)*

The New Testament parallel for *Deuteronomy 6:10-15* is:

> *And having summoned His twelve disciples, He gave them authority over unclean spirits, to cast them out, and to heal every kind of disease and every kind of sickness. . . .These twelve Jesus sent out after instructing them: "As you go preach, saying, 'The kingdom of heaven is at hand.' Heal the sick, raise the dead, cleanse the lepers, cast out demons; freely you received, freely give. Do not acquire gold, or silver, or copper for your money belts, or a bag for your journey, or even two tunics, or sandals, or a staff; for the worker is worthy of his support. And into whatever city or village you enter, inquire who is worthy in it; and abide there until you go away. As you enter the house, give it your greeting. And if the house is worthy, let your greeting of peace come upon it; but if it is not worthy, let your greeting of peace return to you. And whoever does not receive you, nor heed your words, as you go out of that house or city, shake off the dust of your*

Live in Houses You Didn't Build

feet. *Truly I say to you, it will be more tolerable for the land of Sodom and Gomorrah in the day of judgment, than for that city."* (Matthew 10:1-15)

So it is today, 2,000 years later; God's children are STILL *"living in houses they didn't build and eating food they didn't grow."* That's Old and New Testament proof that God does what He says He will do.

I have never seen the righteous forsaken, or his seed begging bread. (Psalm 37:25b)
It is vain for you to rise up early, to retire late, to eat the bread of painful labors; for He gives to His beloved even in his sleep. (Psalm 127:2)

There are also numerous verses concerning the wealth of the wicked that is stored up for the righteous.

For to a person who is good in His sight He has given wisdom and knowledge and joy, while to the sinner He has given the task of gathering and collecting so that he may give to one who is good in God's sight. (Ecclesiastes 2:26)
A good man leaves an inheritance to his children's children, and the wealth of the sinner is stored up for the righteous. (Proverbs 13:22)
Though he piles up silver like dust, and prepares garments as plentiful as the clay; He may prepare it, but the just will wear it. And the innocent will divide the silver. (Job 27:16-17)
And her gain and her harlot's wages will be set apart to the Lord; it will not be stored up or hoarded, but her gain will become sufficient food and choice attire for those who dwell in the presence of the LORD. (Isaiah 23:18)

MIKALA'S RECOLLECTION of GRANDPA'S SAYINGS

Written from Bulgaria when she was a missionary

When you stop to count your blessings, it brings things into perspective. As Grandpa would say, "You never know a man until you have walked a mile in his moccasins." Grandpa didn't say much, except maybe, "Youngun," when we were doing something wrong. But, I am very thankful for all the things that Grandpa, Grandma and Mom taught me:

1. "To work hard."
2. "I didn't beg you to borrow it and I shouldn't have to beg you to get it back."
3. "Always return something in as good, if not better condition than you borrowed it in."
4. "If you break it, buy them a new one."
5. "You are only as good as your word."
6. "Nothing you could ever do would be bad enough to lie about and no one is worth lying to."
7. "A job worth doing is a job worth doing right."
8. "Don't start another project until you finish the first one.
9. "Winners never quit and quitters never win."
10. "Always be thankful."
11. "I was complaining about having no shoes, until I met a man who had no feet." (Grandpa was crippled and in a wheel-chair, however, fought his fight valiantly, setting a very high standard of endurance, and never complaining.)
12. "Fear God, serve God, and give to God. Serve God hard, life is easy; serve God easy and life is hard."

DO YOU WANT TO BE FREE?

Do You WANT out of Prison?

Jesus said it best:
If you forgive men for their transgressions, your heavenly Father will also forgive you. But if you do not forgive men, then your Father will not forgive your transgressions. (Matthew 6:14-15)
That, my brothers and sisters, is what Jesus Christ Himself said at the end of The Lord's Prayer, that we love so much. Forgiveness is not an option; it's a command from our Savior with a consequence. Unforgiveness holds YOU in prison. Don't you WANT to be free? It just can't matter what other people have done to you. Bad stuff has happened to EVERYONE. When you CHOOSE to forgive, it loses its power and then YOUR chains come off. Whether you're in that prison cell or merely the jailer holding someone else in - you're trapped and chained. YOUR sins won't be forgiven if you don't forgive. That's powerful, especially when the Bible says:
ALL have sinned and fall short of the glory of God. (Romans 3:23)
It doesn't say - Y'ALL have sinned - but ALL. That means you haven't done anything I couldn't do and I haven't done anything that you couldn't do. All ground is level at the cross. If I'm to be forgiven, I must forgive others and ask God to forgive me for my sins, and my wrong reaction to offenses. Then, when the devil tries to bring it up again, simply see that person or situation with a FORGIVEN stamp across them. NO EXCEPTIONS. When you CHOOSE to forgive, then YOUR body, mind, soul, and spirit are FREE.
For evil, wherever it's found, always bears within it the seeds of its own destruction; for only in righteousness is there life. Sin always brings death. Turn it all over to God. Let Him judge it because when you do, He won't, but when you won't; He will and He's much more creative.
Never take your own revenge, beloved, but leave room for the wrath of God, for it is written, "VENGEANCE IS MINE, I WILL REPAY," says the Lord. "BUT IF YOUR ENEMY IS HUNGRY, FEED HIM, AND IF HE IS

THIRSTY, GIVE HIM A DRINK; FOR IN SO DOING YOU WILL HEAP BURNING COALS UPON HIS HEAD." Do not be overcome by evil, but overcome evil with good. (Romans 12:19-21)

The standard is, not only must we forgive, but we must also bless. The following are three rules for anyone or anything in our lives:

1. Give thanks for that person or situation, and ask God to help YOU learn everything YOU need to learn THROUGH it. Yes, you're going through - don't camp there - learn what YOU need to learn and go on. It was never about Saul chasing David and hating him; it was about God using that situation to burn the Saul out of David's life. God knows what it takes to make us look more like Jesus and who He will send into our lives to produce the finished product. Whine, cry, or throw a fit, but **GOD IS GOD and We are NOT!** It's not about him, her or them; it's always about you and me. Let's look in the mirror, for there the problem will be looking back at us. It's always the response of our heart that God is watching.
2. Think the best of everyone. Why is it we're so critical of others while we want everyone to see us in our best light? Let's be what WE pretend to be.
3. Love everyone. Trust God to either get them out of your life, or keep them in, but in every situation WE get either bitter or better. It's OUR choice. It's amazing how many people we can love the hell out of, IF we choose to walk like Jesus.

He stood before Pilate and uttered not a word in his own defense *(Matthew 27:14)*. Can we do that? For it's better to know you're right than to have to prove it, because in proving you're right; you become wrong. Is your memory or your vision dictating your life? Get out of the graveyard of your past, throw the shovel away, and walk on. Jesus said, *"Allow the dead to bury their own dead; but as for you, go and proclaim everywhere the kingdom of God...no one, after putting his hand to the plow and looking back, is fit for the kingdom of God."* (Luke 9:60-62)

Do not call to mind the former things, or ponder things of the past. Behold, I will do something new, now it will spring forth; will you not be aware of it? I will even make a roadway in the wilderness, rivers in the desert . . . to

Do You Want to Be FREE?

give drink to My chosen people. The people whom I formed for Myself, will declare My praise. (Isaiah 43:18-21)

The principle of it all is, IF we're living in today, nothing can keep us from praising our God and that's why we were created.

Through Him, then, let us continually offer up a sacrifice of praise to God, that is, the fruit of lips that give thanks to His name. (Hebrews 13:15)

Don't let the devil steal your joy through his tools of unforgiveness and offense. Don't play. Take the poison out and don't chase the snakes of self-pity, resentment, hurt, and ungratefulness. *(See Galatians 5:18-26.)* Whose battle is it anyway? Remember, it was when Moses' brother and sister were picking on him, that God Almighty spoke:

Hear now My words: "If there is a prophet among you, I, the Lord, shall make Myself known to him in a vision. I shall speak with him in a dream. Not so, with My servant Moses, he is faithful in all My household; with him I speak mouth to mouth, even openly, and not in dark sayings, and he beholds the form of the Lord. Why then were you not afraid to speak against My servant, against Moses?" So the anger of the Lord burned against them and He departed. . . .but Miriam was leprous. (Numbers 12:6-10)

I'd say that's a suitable rendition of *"vengeance is Mine, says the Lord."* Just four chapters later, when Korah pulled the same thing - picking on God's anointed - Moses once again gave the Lord plenty of room to show who was HIS:

And Moses said, "By this you shall know that the Lord has sent me to do all these deeds; for this is not my doing. If these men die the death of all men, or if they suffer the fate of all men, then the Lord has not sent me. But if the Lord brings about an entirely new thing and the ground opens its mouth and swallows them up with all that is theirs, and they descend alive into Sheol, then you will understand that these men have spurned the Lord." Then it came about as he finished speaking all these words, that the ground that was under them split open; and the earth opened its mouth and swallowed them up, and their households and all the men who belonged to Korah with their possessions. (Numbers 16:28-32)

As you can see, God doesn't have a shortage of power for HIS vengeance; what He has, is a shortage of people who will let HIM do the vengeance instead of themselves. God said:

"No weapon that is formed against you shall prosper; and every tongue that accuses you in judgment you will condemn. This is the heritage of the servants of the Lord, and their vindication is from ME," declares the Lord. (Isaiah 54:17)

So, why don't we let the God of the Universe fight our battles and vindicate us? Is it because it's so hard to keep our mouths shut, our hands clean, and our hearts pure? The cure for being offended is - GROW UP. If you have time to be offended, you have too much time on your hands. Ask God for a project to do for Him, to keep you out of trouble. It's real simple - dead soldiers don't bleed. When you choose to take no offense the devil can't bug you AND God takes over. Remember whose battle it is. David, a man after God's own heart knew:

"You come to me with a sword, a spear, and a javelin, but I come to you in the name of the Lord of hosts, the God of the armies of Israel, whom you have taunted. This day the Lord will deliver you up into my hands, and I will strike you down and remove your head from you. And I will give the dead bodies of the army of the Philistines this day to the birds of the sky and the wild beasts of the earth, that all the earth may know that there is a God in Israel and that all this assembly may know that the Lord does not deliver by sword or by spear; for the battle is the Lord's and He will give you into our hands.". . .David RAN quickly toward the battle. (1 Samuel 17:45-48)

The rest is history. The kid (David) winds up with a giant's head in his hands. It's merely a test and when we pass it, we'll get promoted to the next test, and the next, until we meet Jesus. We can choose to live victoriously over everything that comes our way. Choose to look beyond the obstacle that's looming in front of you trying to block your way. RUN around it. Your victory is on the other side. Don't stop. Go forth in victory, shoving devils aside, praising your God!

BROKENNESS - 101

The course no one signs up for

Brokenness 101: Although few willingly sign up for it, we don't see God without it. You'd think the **GOD IS GOD and We are NOT** part would go without saying, but isn't it the LORDSHIP of Jesus Christ that we fight against the most? While many acknowledge Him as Savior, it seems few will call Him LORD. Is that why we gripe and complain and shake our fist at God? Because if WE were GOD, we'd have this thing lined out so sweetly that NO adversity or person would bug us. However, God is holy and He's looking for people who will worship Him and love Him in and through...ALL things.

Paul could say at the end of his journey: *Not that I speak from want; for I have learned to be content in whatever circumstances I am.* (Philippians 4:11) We should try considering the things Paul endured and that he shared with us in *2 Corinthians 11:23-33*, lest we complain too much.

Beloved, do not be surprised at the fiery ordeal among you, which comes upon you for your testing, as though some strange thing were happening to you. (1 Peter 4:12)

Brothers and sisters, that's what this life is all about, this trial run for heaven. IF we praise Him here, we get to praise Him forever. Truly, He is Lord of ALL or not at all. It seems David BECAME a man after God's own heart. God knows what it takes for the becoming because HE IS and will always be the potter. We'll never be anything but the **clay** part.

Woe to the one who quarrels with his Maker--an earthenware vessel among the vessels of earth. Will the clay say to the potter, "What are you doing?" Or the thing you are making say, "He has no hands?" (Isaiah 45:9)

What audacity! Try reading through chapters 32-42 of the book of Job to get God's perspective of all this, especially Chapter 33.

Behold, let me tell you, you are not right in this. For God is greater than man. Why do you complain against Him, that He does not give account of all His doings? Indeed, God speaks once, or twice, yet no one notices it.

GOD IS GOD and We are NOT!

In a dream, a vision of the night, when sound sleep falls on men, while they slumber in their beds, then He opens the ears of men and seals their instruction, that He may turn aside man from his conduct, and keep man from pride. . . .Man is also chastened with pain on his bed. . . .If there is an angel as mediator for him, one out of a thousand, to remind a man what is right for him. . . .Then he will pray to God, and He will accept him, that he may see His face with joy. (Job 33:12-26)

Remember that God sits in the heavens and does what pleases Him. (See *Psalm 2*.)

One night as I was taking my eight-year-old nephew home from a restaurant in his hometown, I asked, "Adam, how do we get to your house from here?"

He, very innocently, answered, "Well, I don't know Aunt Barbara, my mom or dad always drive."

I thought, how simple. All little Adam does is sit in the car and KNOW, without a shadow of doubt, that his parents will take him where he needs to go with NO concern on his part. That's their job. Why don't we do that with our heavenly Father who made this whole show and keeps it going? CHILL does seem to be the password into this walk with the Lord.

It's like God is the dad driving the truck and we are the kids who get to ride in the back and eat our Popsicle's. BUT sometimes we want to crawl through that window, take over, and drive. However, **GOD IS GOD and We are NOT!** He knows what it takes to make us usable - to make us "keepers." The bottom-line is, what have we done for Him, and how much do we look like His dear Son?

So, Father God, turn up the heat and burn out everything that doesn't look like Jesus - and also Lord - when we start yelling and screaming about that too-hot fire, don't listen because we know that You know what You're doing, because **YOU are GOD and We are NOT!**

When we really understand that God is sovereign, we'll learn to walk that servant and his master story in *Luke 17:7-10,* knowing we're just supposed to do what we're hired to do - be God's kids and SERVE. Then we can just love everyone through our tests because we know that God has them in our lives to produce His best in us, and that they can't do anything He doesn't allow.

And we know that God causes all things to work together for good to those who love God, to those who are called according to His purpose. (Romans 8:28)
It's just a test, merely a test and when we pass it with clean hands and a pure heart, WE are promoted. Nothing is worth being stuck or stopped. We have to look beyond the people, places and things and just be sure that WE are about our Father's business because one day that's all that's going to matter.

"Even though these three men, Noah, Daniel, and Job were in its midst, by their own righteousness they could only deliver themselves," declares the Lord God. (Ezekiel 14:14,16,18,20)

We are our only problem. If, however, we signed up for the test through sin, then we must repent, change and ask God for His solution. There are some things that God allows to "make a believer" out of us, and assure that we will NEVER walk that way again. End of discussion. Thank You, Lord, for your grace, forgiveness, love, and mercy and for being the God of second chances that King David knew so well. *(1 Samuel 15--2 Samuel 24:25)*

Have you lost your peace? Go back to where you lost it. Repent for your presumptuous words and deeds and:

Fall on the Rock and be broken, so the rock doesn't fall on you and you be crushed. (See Luke 20:18)

God never said it'd be easy, but He said, that He would be with us. And guess what? Dead soldiers don't bleed, nor do they murmur or complain. So, if the YOU in you is throwing a fit, tell your head, your heart, and your whiny self to be still and KNOW God. Praise God in and through ALL things. THAT shows you're a King's kid. He doesn't have to pamper our flesh. It has to die so the God in us can live. Amen and Amen.

You are a King's kid and the devil is a liar. Let God, Jehovah, be exalted in you and in me, today. Hallelujah. What you can see is not real, but what you can't see...THAT is real.

While we look not at the things which are seen, but at the things which are not seen; for the things which are

seen are temporal, but the things which are not seen are eternal. (2 Corinthians. 4:18)
Even God, who gives life to the dead and calls into being that which does not exist. (Romans. 4:17)
For we walk by faith, not by sight. (2 Corinthians. 5:7)
There is also the charge in Isaiah 42:18-19:
Hear, you deaf. And look, you blind, that you may see. Who is blind but My servant, or so deaf as My messenger whom I send? Who is so blind as he that is at peace with Me, or so blind as the servant of the Lord?

Will we be blind to be God's servant? Will we be deaf to be His messenger? The positions are open, for "all who will, to come." There are lots of vacancies for servants who will walk with Him today. Paul said, *"Work out YOUR salvation with fear and trembling."* (Philippians 2:12b)

The Lord said to Jeremiah, *"IF you return, then I will restore you—before Me you will stand; and IF you extract the precious from the worthless, you will become MY spokesman. They for their part may turn to you, but as for you, you must not turn to them."* (Jeremiah 15:19)

To stand before God, and be His spokesman, is worth more than ANYTHING this world has to offer. YES, YES, my Lord, my God and my King. It's our choice. God always said IF - IF you will extract the precious from the worthless. That means in today's English, get the junk out.

One day, as I was praying in my office, trying to FIND God, I had a vision. In it I had bills, advertising schedules, orders, the children, all this stuff in my hands so I couldn't lift them up to praise God. Then, God, in His mercy, began drawing me into His presence and my hands began to rise up and praise Him. The junk that was in them turned to slime and melted down my arms. In the presence of the King nothing can stand.

So Lord, once again turn up the heat and burn everything out that stands between You and me today. Thank You, Lord, that Your grace is sufficient. Hallelujah, this hurts so good. Truly there is grace for going THROUGH. God is jealous and He will not share His glory with another. It's usually the thing we hold onto so tightly and bargain with God about - you know, the **everything but this Lord.** However, He comes in as Lord and in His lordship position has full authority to remove anything that blocks our view of Him. Only He knows how the tapestry of our life is supposed to look, sometimes we see only the knots. That's why **HE is GOD and We are NOT!**

The hard cruel fact is that some just may not make it. Beyond what God has anointed us to deal with, we have to turn everything over to Him. We're not here to be little gods to other people. One thing I'm learning is that the worst place to be is between God and someone He's breaking because He will allow you to be broken through that situation to get you out of the way so HE can accomplish HIS good purpose in each of the lives. The quicker we quit, the sooner the other person will hear the voice of God. Then the blame won't fall on us. AMEN and AMEN. So again, **GOD IS GOD and We are NOT!** Hallelujah. Keep going Christian. It's not so bad being fired from everyone's life but your own. Be fired and let **GOD be GOD!**

Paul warns that worldly sorrow leads to death while godly sorrow leads to repentance and life. (See *2 Corinthians 7:8-10.*)

The focus is to keep clean hands and a pure heart during our journey THROUGH because that's the only way we'll see God, or get to ascend the hill of the Lord *(Psalm 24:3).* Besides, it's just a test, merely a test, and when you pass it you'll get promoted to the NEXT test. The righteous live by faith, believing in the unseen hand of the LIVING God to bring them through ALL their tests and storms victoriously, abundantly blessed. Remember when the three Hebrew boys told the king:

Let it be known to you, O King, that we are not going to serve your gods or worship the golden image you have set up. (Daniel 3:18)

Sure they signed themselves up for a fire, BUT, there was a fourth man, the Son of God, in that fire with them and ALL they lost were their chains. However, the guys who threw them in lost their lives. So, once again, the fire isn't a bad place to be, it's a SAFE place. No one could bother them in there. *(See Daniel 3.)* Just be very sure that the Son of God is in there with you and ALL you'll lose are your chains. Besides, who wants chains anyway? I'm sure that no overcoming child of the LIVING GOD does.

About midnight Paul and Silas were praying and singing hymns of praise to God, and the prisoners were listening to them; and suddenly there came a great earthquake, so that the foundations of the prison house were shaken; and immediately all the doors were opened, and everyone's chains were unfastened. (Acts 16:25-26)

One day, Joseph awoke in the prison BUT he went to bed in the palace *(Genesis 41)*. Moses spent forty years becoming something, then forty years being broken to nothing, only to spend his last forty years with God, showing what HE could do with nothing *(Exodus 3)*. Doesn't the God of the Universe hang the sun, moon, and stars on nothing? So Body of Christ, let's get grateful in ALL things for God knows what we need. The breaking wasn't Saul's. It was about David and his heart being purged and purified so that one day it could be said of him that he was a man after God's own heart *(Acts 13:22)*.

For one day we shall hand the book of our life back to God. Above all we want to hear Jesus say, *"Well done, My good and faithful servant; you were faithful with a few things, I will put you in charge of many things, enter into the joy of your master" (Matthew 25:21, 23)*. We have today. What will we do with it that will count for eternity?

Lord, I pray for the body of Christ today, that You bring each one through the storms of their lives victoriously. That You bless each reader with fresh hope, OH GOD, hope that there's a new day coming. Let them know they're free to go onward and upward with You. Thank you for that blessed assurance of knowing that You're in charge, and You'll never let the fire get too hot, just hot enough to burn up everything that can't stand in Your presence, so the captives can go free, to owe no man anything but the love of Jesus Christ. God, we repent of every sin against You and the people in our lives, and ask for forgiveness and change, that those streams of refreshing will come. We want to be holy vessels that can be used for Your honor and glory. Do whatever it takes, sweet Jesus, to make us more like You. We praise and thank You, Lord. To You belongs all the honor and glory, forever and ever. Amen and Amen.

QUIT BEGGING FOR CURSES

Gossip, the tongue and other defiled things

Solomon, touted as the wisest man spoke these words concerning the tongue:

With the fruit of a man's mouth his stomach will be satisfied; he will be satisfied with the product of his lips. Death and life are in the power of the tongue, and those who love it will eat its fruit. (Proverbs 18:20-21)

Do not be hasty in word or impulsive in thought to bring up a matter in the presence of God. For God is in heaven and you are on the earth; therefore let your words be few. Do not let your speech cause you to sin and do not say in the presence of the messenger of God that it was a mistake. Why should God be angry on account of your voice and destroy the work of your hands? (Ecclesiastes 5:2, 6)

How is it that Samuel had a 100% anointing?

Thus Samuel grew and the Lord was with him and let none of his words fail. (1 Samuel 3:19)

My best guess is that he kept his mouth shut UNLESS God told him what to speak. How often do we clutter up the spiritual and the natural realm with our garbage - defending, judging, criticizing, murmuring, and complaining?

Jesus said, "Either make the tree good, and its fruit good; or make the tree bad, and its fruit bad; for the tree is known by its fruit. You brood of vipers, how can you, being evil, speak what is good? For the mouth speaks out of that which fills the heart. The good man out of his good treasure brings forth what is good; and the evil man out of his evil treasure brings forth what is evil. And I say to you, that every careless word that men shall speak, they shall render account for it in the day of judgment. For by your words you shall be justified, and by your words, you shall be condemned." (Matthew 12:33-37)

That's a rather serious statement from our Lord. Listen to your words.

> *Let your yes be yes, and your no, no; so that you may not fall under judgment. (James 5:12b)*

If we don't have anything nice to say we shouldn't say anything at all, for one day we will give account for the words we've spoken. Have you ever tape-recorded your conversations and listened to them? You could have your own personal dress rehearsal to see whether you're speaking life or death over the situations you're involved in.

Another good standard to set for our tongue is to talk TO people and not ABOUT them. This will accomplish at least two things - you WILL change the way you talk, and you'll also give the other person the benefit of getting to address your criticisms. Gossip takes two equally guilty parties, ears and a mouth. Once the Lord told me what a houseguest had been saying about me. I went to the guest and said, "God said you've talked ABOUT me. Would you like to talk TO me?" When the church of Jesus Christ gets filled with the HOLY Spirit, this game is going to stop.

> *James said, "If anyone thinks himself to be religious, and yet does not bridle his tongue but deceives his own heart, this man's religion is worthless." (James 1:26)*

> *If anyone does not stumble in what he says, he is a perfect man, able to bridle the whole body as well. . . So also the tongue is a small part of the body, and yet it boasts of great things. Behold, how great a forest is set aflame by such a small fire. And the tongue is a fire, the very world of iniquity; the tongue is set among our members as that which defiles the entire body, and sets on fire the course of our life, and is set on fire by hell. For every species of beasts and birds, of reptiles and creatures of the sea, is tamed, and has been tamed by the human race. But no one can tame the tongue; it is a restless evil and full of deadly poison. With it we bless our Lord and Father; and with it we curse men, who have been made in the likeness of God; from the same mouth come both blessing and cursing. My brethren, these things ought not to be this way. (James 3:2,5-10)*

Not only will we be judged by all we've said but also while we're talking trash, God can't put His words in our mouth. He's looking for people that will die to their own thoughts and words in order to speak HIS words. Elihu said it very well:

Let me speak that I may get relief; let me open my lips and answer. Let me now be partial to no one; nor flatter any man. For I do not know how to flatter, else my Maker would soon take me away. (Job 32:20-22)

Jesus said, "For I did not speak on My own initiative, but the Father Himself who sent Me has given Me commandment, what to say, and what to speak. And I know that His commandment is eternal life; therefore the things I speak, I speak just as the Father has told Me. (John 12:49-50)

Will we do that? Will we hold our peace and only speak what the Father is speaking? That's one way to die to ourselves as Jesus did before Pilate *(Matthew 27:11-18)* when He uttered not a word in His own defense. Can we do that? Can we have nothing to defend, nothing to debate, and nothing to judge?

Not returning evil for evil, or insult for insult, but giving a blessing instead; for you were called for the very purpose that you might inherit a blessing. For, let him who means to love life and see good days refrain his tongue from evil and his lips from speaking guile. (1 Peter 3:9-10)

Jesus said, "Everyone therefore who shall confess Me before men, I will also confess him before My Father who is in heaven. But whoever shall deny Me before men, I will also deny him before My Father Who is in heaven." (Matthew 10:32-33)

Think of it, while we're confessing Jesus to someone, He's confessing us to the Father. Now, brothers and sisters, that's some good press. We're always lifting up something or someone in our speech - the games, the latest fashion, whatever stuff our flesh happens to be into that day. However, only God knows if we're the last chance that person has to hear the gospel of Jesus Christ and if so, what did we do with our opportunity for a divine appointment? Jesus said, *"If I be lifted up. . .I will draw all men to Myself." (John 12:32)*

We must be lifting up Jesus - that's all that counts. God sends His children across the paths of many hurting people each day. We have the answer, but do we give it? There's nothing benefited by giving the world, the flesh, or ourselves to anyone. The ONLY way we can build up those we meet is by giving them JESUS. One day that's all that will count. Store up those days now.

And there must be no filthiness and silly talk or coarse jesting, which are not fitting, but rather giving of thanks. (Ephesians 5:4)

We were created to praise our God. And we are praising our GOD or our god. Just listen and you'll know.

Through Him then, let us continually offer up a sacrifice of praise to God, that is, the fruit of lips that give thanks to His name. (Hebrews 13:15)

The other part about the tongue is that murmuring and complaining can sign you up for another lap in the wilderness, just like it did the Israelites. *(See Numbers 11.)*

Now the people became like those who complain of adversity in the hearing of the Lord; and when the Lord heard it, His anger was kindled, and the fire of the Lord burned among them and consumed some of the outskirts of the camp. But on the next day all the congregation of the sons of Israel grumbled against Moses and Aaron. . .and the Lord spoke to Moses, saying, "Get away from this congregation, that I may consume them instantly." (Numbers 16:21,45)

God isn't playing on this issue. He knows where we are and until we praise Him in ALL things, they just aren't going to change. Let's repent, change, begin again and be found praising our God. Will we respond to our tests as lights in a dark world, OR, when tests come will we yell and scream louder than the sinner? If we're screaming, WHY should the sinner want our God? God needs LIGHTS in this dark world, praising God - LIGHTS.

Work out your salvation with fear and trembling; for it is God who is at work in you, both to will and to work for His good pleasure. Do ALL things without grumbling or disputing; that you may prove yourselves to be blameless and innocent, children of God above reproach in the midst of a crooked and perverse generation, among whom you appear as lights in the world. (Philippians 2:12b-15)

MARRIAGE

Battleground or Blessing?

MARRIAGE brings to every couple a basket of puzzle pieces, his pieces and her pieces, that must be meshed together to create a union that is truly one flesh. The guide for putting it all together is The Holy Bible; reading and obeying it brings the blessing of success. The work God gives to a husband and wife is to pray for and seek His guidance and leading to fashion a union that will bring honor and glory to the One who said:

> It is not good for the man to be alone; I will make him a helper suitable for him. *(Genesis 2:18)*

A helper to build up and not tear down, to serve and love as unto the Lord. Jesus said the greatest would be the servant of all. *(Luke 22:26)* How much we love Jesus is always shown by how much we are loving that mate He gave us. He gave Himself and called us to do likewise. Here's the story…

> The Lord God fashioned into a woman the rib, which He had taken from the man, and brought her to the man. And the man said, "This is now bone of my bones, and flesh of my flesh; she shall be called Woman, because she was taken out of Man."
>
> For this cause a man shall leave his father and his mother, and shall cleave to his wife; and they shall become one flesh. And the man and his wife were both naked and were not ashamed. *(Genesis 2:22-25)*

One problem I've seen destroy marriages is when one partner is not willing to leave his/her father or mother in order to cleave to his/her spouse. It's interesting to me that before Adam or Eve even had parents, to set a standard for how marriage would work, God said to leave that important parental relationship and cleave to your spouse. Your marriage is your business; no one else's! Pull together…repent, forgive, bless and PRAY for each other, building up God's plan for you.

We'll begin with *1 Peter 2:21-25*, to lay the foundation for the Biblical marriage scenario found in *1 Peter 3*:

> *For you have been called for this purpose, since Christ also suffered for you, leaving you an example for you to follow in His steps, who committed no sin, nor was any deceit found in His mouth; and while being reviled, He did not revile in return; while suffering, He uttered no threats, but kept entrusting Himself to Him who judges righteously; and He Himself bore our sins in His body on the cross, that we might die to sin and live to righteousness; for by His wounds you were healed. For you were continually straying like sheep, but now you have returned to the Shepherd and Guardian of your souls.*

Now for the likewises that follow…First to the wives:

> *Likewise, (in the same way) you wives, be submissive to your own husbands so that even if any of them are disobedient to the word, they may be won WITHOUT A WORD by the behavior of their wives, as they observe your CHASTE AND RESPECTFUL BEHAVIOR. And let not your adornment be merely external—braiding the hair, and wearing gold jewelry, or putting on dresses; but let it be the hidden person of the heart, with the imperishable quality of a GENTLE AND QUIET SPIRIT, which is precious in the sight of God. For in this way in former times the holy women also, who hoped in God, used to adorn themselves, being submissive to their own husbands. Thus Sarah obeyed Abraham, calling him lord, and you have become her children if you do what is right without being frightened by any fear. (1 Peter 3:1-6)*

Women, the word to us is SUBMIT. That was the biggest word I'd heard in my life. But we as holy women today must cleanse ourselves of the Jezebel spirits (See 1 Kings18-21) that would belittle the men God has given us, then resent them for

Marriage...Battleground or Blessing?

being the wimps we've made them. My sisters, it shouldn't be this way, not for God's women. We have to repent, change, and humble ourselves in the sight of the Lord - and in due season - He will exalt us.

> *A wise woman builds her house, but the foolish tears it down with her own hands. (Proverbs 14:1)*

Let's act saved. Let's love and serve as unto the Lord and be quiet. Think the best of and be grateful for those men God has given us. Those are not choices. That's God's way of you being blessed under the covering He's given you. God knows how to straighten that man out. You've been fired - you don't have to do it. **GOD IS GOD and We are NOT!** God will defend and protect you and your children. He knows how to break and humble both men and women to make them more like Jesus. Our part is to pray and get out of the way. Let **GOD be GOD!**

My late husband's biggest prayer was, "God, change me to love Barbara like she needs to be loved." I can assure you, God will move heaven, earth and hell to answer prayers like that. Can we or will we pray that for our spouses? Remember that it's never the other person that God's concerned with. It's the one you see in the mirror looking back at you.

Now, to the husbands:

> *You husbands likewise, live with your wives in an understanding way, as with a weaker vessel, since she is a woman; and grant her honor as a fellow heir of the grace of life, so that YOUR PRAYERS MAY NOT BE HINDERED. To sum up, let all be harmonious, sympathetic, brotherly, kindhearted, and humble in spirit; not returning evil for evil, or insult for insult, but giving a blessing instead; for you were called for the very purpose that you might inherit a blessing. (1 Peter 3:7-9)*

What you give out, will come back. It's said that opposites attract. *Iron sharpens iron. (Proverbs 27:17)* No, he's not you and you're not him, but you're each what the other needs to become more like Jesus. Remember, it's a test, merely a test.

In becoming one flesh, God gives preeminence to our physical union, and so should we.

> The husband should fulfill his marital duty to his wife, and likewise the wife to her husband. The wife's body does not belong to her alone but also to her husband. In the same way, the husband's body does not belong to him alone but also to his wife. Do not deprive each other, except by mutual consent and for a time, so that you may devote yourselves to prayer. Then come together again so that Satan will not tempt you because of your lack of self-control. (1 Corinthians 7:3-5)

Lovemaking is God's gift to a husband and wife; the greatest tranquilizer known to man. Only within the bounds of HOLY matrimony can God bless the union that He and all the angels cheer on. This good plan for His kids has no guilt or shame; it's pure and holy.

> Let marriage be held in honor among all, and let the marriage bed be undefiled; for fornicators and adulterers God will judge. (Hebrews 13:4)

The second part of that scripture; fornication and adultery, bears within it the seeds of its own destruction. Only in righteousness is there life, sin always leads to death. God has NO EXCEPTIONS to His rules.

> Jesus said, "Have you not read, that He who created them from the beginning made them male and female, and said, 'For this cause a man shall leave his father and mother, and shall cleave to his wife; and the two shall become one flesh?' Consequently they are no longer two, but one flesh. What therefore God has joined together, let no man separate."
>
> They said to Him, "Why then did Moses command to give her a certificate and divorce her?" He said to them, "Because of your hardness of heart, Moses permitted you to divorce your wives; but from the beginning it has not

Marriage...Battleground or Blessing?

been this way. And I say to you, whoever divorces his wife, except for immorality, and marries another woman commits adultery." (Matthew 19:4-9)

Men and women, we can take God easy or we can take Him hard, but GOD is going to win. Sometimes it's just a matter of **how low can you go?** Before you give up and do it His way, to live and to love according to His principles, the ones that have His blessings.

The Lord lays out His standard in the Word:

For the husband is the head of the wife as Christ also is the head of the church, He Himself being the Savior of the body, but as the church is subject to Christ, so also the wives ought to be to their husbands in everything. Husbands, love your wives, just as Christ also loved the church and gave Himself up for her; that He might sanctify her, having cleansed her by the washing of water with the Word, that He might present to Himself the church in all her glory, having no spot or wrinkle or any such thing; but that she should be holy and blameless.

So, husbands ought to love their own wives as their own bodies. He who loves his own wife loves himself; for no one ever hated his own flesh, but nourishes and cherishes it, just as Christ also does the church, because we are members of His body. FOR THIS CAUSE A MAN SHALL LEAVE HIS FATHER AND MOTHER, AND SHALL CLEAVE TO HIS WIFE; AND THE TWO SHALL BECOME ONE FLESH. This mystery is great; but I am speaking with reference to Christ and the church. Nevertheless let each individual among you also love his own wife, even as himself; and let the wife see to it that she respect her husband. (Ephesians 5:22-33)

An interesting note here is that God commanded **men to love** (knowing that would be their hard part) and **women to submit** (knowing that would be their tough part). So He spelled it out, **JUST DO IT.** Pretty clear, isn't it? That's a command; we just don't have any choices. Men, you are accountable before the church, and died for it. God for your wife and family. So love your wife as Jesus loved

Another scripture to consider is *Malachi 2:13-16:*

You cover the altar of the Lord with tears, with weeping and with groaning, because He no longer regards the offering or accepts it with favor from your hand. Yet you say, "For what reason?" Because the Lord has been a witness between you and the wife of your youth, against whom you have dealt treacherously, though she is your companion and your wife by covenant. But not one has done so who has a remnant of the Spirit. And what did that one do while he was seeking a godly offspring?

Take heed then to your spirit and let no one deal treacherously against the wife of your youth. "For I hate divorce," says the Lord, the God of Israel, "and him who covers his garment with wrong," says the Lord of hosts. "So take heed to your spirit, that you do not deal treacherously."

"I'm not in love." Oh please. Love is a choice and you have a covenant before a holy God. It's a command; act in love and the feelings will follow. What did you do when you were dating and **in love?** Do those same caring, loving things again. God is a God of miracles and there were three in the covenant on that wedding day of I DO'S.

Jesus said, "What I have joined together, let no man separate." (Matthew 19:6)

That means, let not you or anyone else, separate. The grass isn't greener on the other side, it's just new and different. But in the end the lawn still needs cutting, unless it's Astroturf, then it's plastic and not real. The devil is a liar and the father of all lies. He has a lot of cheap imitations out there but he never tells you what the payday is. We're free to make our choices, HOWEVER, we're not free from the consequences of those choices.

And no wonder, for even Satan disguises himself as an angel of light. (2 Corinthians 11:14)

There are wolves in sheep's clothing sent out to kill, steal, and destroy the good work God has begun. Read *Proverbs 5-7* to get your head straight concerning this issue. Go ahead and read it; get the truth and it WILL set you free. Never have I counseled a man or a woman who's fallen and been told the experience was what the devil painted it to be. Hell is hell and the wages of sin is death. God's word is clear and is true.

God is shaking and breaking all the ungodly qualities from our hearts to make us more like His dear Son. He's the potter and we are but clay for Him to mold and make as He sees fit. He hasn't missed a beat. He's still, *"Causing ALL things to work together for good to those who love God, to those who are called according to HIS purpose." (Romans 8:28)*

God is looking for couples who will die to themselves, their flesh and their pride, who will put aside strife and contention. Couples who will build up one another in love and fulfill the call of God on their lives. With a world out there dying and going to hell there's just no time left for Christian couples to be fighting internal wars of division and contention. Pray for peace and unity in your home and endeavor to walk with a single vision for the purposes of God, onward and upward. Paddle that boat in the same direction. Trust God to fight your battles for He is able.

He who began a good work in you will perfect it until the day of Christ Jesus. (Philippians 1:6b)

Repent for the hate, anger, bitterness, judgments, stubbornness and rebellion in your own heart. Ask God to change YOU to become the husband or wife God wants you to be. Love as Jesus loved. Serve as He served wanting no rewards or accolades.

Jesus explained it very clearly in *Luke 17:7-10:*

But which of you, having a slave plowing or tending sheep, will say to him when he has come in from the field, "Come immediately and sit down to eat?" But will he not say to him, "Prepare something for me to eat, and properly clothe yourself and serve me until I have eaten and drunk; and afterward you will eat and drink?" He does not thank the slave because he did the things which were commanded, does he? So you too, when you do all the things which are commanded you, say, "We are unworthy slaves; we have done only that which we ought to have done."

Does it sound tough brothers and sisters? Jesus never said it'd be easy but He said that He'd be with us. So what if it's a thankless job? Did you ever ask God to use you? Well, when

He does, why complain? Our reward is in heaven and God is watching. When we are faithful in little THEN we will be given much. So what if we have to piggyback them to heaven? What if you were the only Christian your spouse ever saw? Would he/she want the Jesus you profess? Jesus was meek and humble. He never pushed Himself on anyone and neither can we. If we don't, HE will. God will either get people right or remove them from our lives, but it can't be our decision. Patiently we wait on the Lord and we walk into *Isaiah 40:31:*

Yet those who wait for the Lord will gain new strength; they will mount up with wings like eagles, they will run and not get tired, they will walk and not become weary.

When a man's ways are pleasing to the Lord, He makes even his enemies to be at peace with him. (Proverbs 16:7)

God WILL show. He showed with Abigail's husband, Nabal:

And about ten days later, it happened that the Lord struck Nabal, and he died. (1 Samuel 25:38)

Our heart has to always be for God's best in our spouses' life, and as we pray blessings upon them we'll be blessed. **GOD IS GOD and We are NOT!** We don't know what makes people do the things they do but as God's children we must be found loving, thinking the best of, and being grateful for the mates the Lord has given us. It just may be the greatest test of YOUR Christianity. Will you not judge, not defend yourself, and not be critical - so YOU will be changed through the process? The fire always makes the gold purer and only God knows how hot it has to be to burn the junk out of OUR lives. We don't want to be found fighting against the very hand of God.

Try reading *Psalm 91*, AGAIN:

He who dwells in the shelter of the Most High will abide in the shadow of the Almighty. I will say to the Lord, "My refuge and my fortress, My God, in whom I trust. . . ."

Keep reading.

Nothing is worth strife and division in a home so QUIT IT. Any game is over when SOMEONE quits playing. NO ONE can make you play stupid games. Trust God to fight your battles and to change hearts, beginning with yours. It's better to know you're right than to have to prove it, for in proving it, (defending yourself) you become wrong. Quit whining and complaining.

Marriage...Battleground or Blessing?

Stop wallowing in self-pity and wanting to live on a pedestal, instead love and serve as unto Jesus. Show daily how much you love your Lord by how much you're loving your mate.

We love, because He first loved us. If someone says, "I love God," and hates his brother, he is a liar; for the one who does not love his brother whom he has seen, cannot love God whom he has not seen. And this commandment we have from Him, that the one who loves God should love his brother also. (John 4:20-21)

We have to put our personal preferences aside in order to live in peace, and make a difference in this world. We must love Jesus first, next our mates, our children and then go love a lost and dying world, telling them of a Savior, Who gave His life for them. We must be about our Father's business because that's ALL that will matter throughout eternity. So, child of the Most High God, can you? Will you love and serve by the standard Christ set, giving Himself for so many? Be blessed.

P.S. I've walked as a divorcee, a wife and a widow...and I thank God that He's a God of second, third, fourth (however many you need)....chances. The remnant seems to be made mostly of those who needed a couple of tries to get it right. If you've fallen or failed; repent and BE FORGIVEN. (1 John 1:9) Let go of your past and walk forward, trusting the God of the Universe to pick up all those pieces and make something not only useable, but also beautiful out of whatever mess is behind you. Keep walking. God loves you. He has a plan and it only gets better from here. God is putting together powerhouses to work for Him these days. I'd rather have taken a few turns in the road than to still be sitting around judging everyone else and wondering what the Blood of Jesus is all about. His judgement was MERCY!

The Defiled Bride

Church, where is your HOLINESS?

Church; let's get right on with this holiness issue. Some sanctify sloppy agape. However, if they were to visit Jerusalem they would notice that a fence still separates the men from the women at the Wailing Wall, even today. The church cannot condone fleshly indulgences. Pastors, take care in counseling women. Women, resist the desire to help "that poor brother" in the Lord. *Your adversary, the devil, prowls about like a roaring lion, seeking whom he may devour.* (1 Peter 5:8) Never let the covering of Christ be an excuse to indulge in the flesh.

As obedient children, do not be conformed to the former lusts which were yours in your ignorance, but like the Holy One who called you, be holy yourselves also in all your behavior, because it is written, "You shall be holy, for I am HOLY." (1 Peter 1:14-16)

GOD said that. Pretty clear, isn't it? Guys deal with guys and girls deal with girls. That sets a standard of holiness for the church which keeps out flesh treats and spiritual adultery. Don't forget, it was GOD who said, *"Be HOLY as I am HOLY."* If it seems harsh, just know that sloppy agape wasn't God's idea.

Paul said in *1 Corinthians 6:19-20* and *7:1-2:*

Or do you not know that your body is a temple of the Holy Spirit who is in you, whom you have from God, and that you are not your own? For you have been bought with a price; therefore glorify God in your body. Now concerning the things about which you wrote, it is good for a man not to touch a woman. But because of immoralities, let each man have his own wife, and let each woman have her own husband.

Husbands and wives, above the friends you each have in the Lord, God gave you one another to be his/her best friend. Marriage is that God-given relationship of protection for each of you. It calls the con on any games or set-ups from hell. I feel that Craig Landfair in his song, <u>NOBODY FROM NOWHERE,</u> says it very well:

The Defiled Bride

Tell me where are you from, what do you do,
Have you been to school? Who do you know,
What can you show, to tell me some more about you?
Well, I'm just nobody from nowhere
And I'm learning not to care,
What those somebody's from somewhere got to say.
I'm just nobody from nowhere but that's just all right with me
'Cause on a stormy night, I lost my life on a hill called Calvary.
Well, I'm nobody from nowhere
I've got a taste of destiny
'Cause He's taken me to where us nobody's from nowhere
Can fly free.
I don't drive a Mercedes or chase pretty ladies
I've got a woman for my life and she stands by my side
To keep me from pride, I've found a very good wife.
No BMW will never say that I love you
Like my little boy's shining eyes. Hey, I don't own a condo,
But there's something I do know
All that glitters simply isn't gold.
Blind men play the flute and the people start to dance
But I'm standing here alone
I hear the wind blow and where it comes I don't know
But I'll keep stretching out my wings
'Cause I'm nobody from nowhere
BUT I'M FREE.

    Craig wrote that song while driving a bus full of teen-agers home from youth camp. He was just thanking God for his lot in life.

    As Mikala's youth pastor, he shared the following story with the youth group that helped many of them stay pure.

    One of the girls had been unmercifully harassed at her college dorm because of her purity. Finally, tired of the harassment she replied, "I could go out tonight and become as you are, but you could never be like me again." Her response seemed to settle the issue, HOLINESS WILL PREVAIL!

    I praise God for the ones He delivers from drugs, impurities, the lusts of the flesh, immorality and the various traps from hell. But too often I think we fail to hear of, or to give thanks for, those He KEEPS pure and holy. That's the bride Jesus is coming back to receive, a kept and chaste bride, holy as He is Holy.

I urge you therefore, brethren, by the mercies of God, to present your bodies a living and holy sacrifice, acceptable to God which is your spiritual service of worship. And do not be conformed to this world, but be transformed by the renewing of your mind, that you may prove what the will of God is, that which is good and acceptable and perfect." (Romans 12:1-2)

Paul is warning not to be **conned** into the form of this world, *conformed to this world*, instead renew your mind. Let's let go of the vision of this world and take on *"Thy Kingdom come, Thy will be done, on earth as it is in Heaven."* (Matthew 6:10)

Father God, I pray for each reader a prayer of healing in their innermost being. For your daughter, Lord, I ask you to heal and deliver her. Set her free from the use and abuse at the hands of men. Oh God, in Your mercy and love, put her in Your lap, put Your big arms around her and love her back to health I pray.

For Your son, mighty God, I ask you to set him free from the condemnation, rejections and fears that keep him from being the mighty man of God you've called him to be. Set him free from the chains and games that women have put upon him so he can freely hear the call you gave to Gideon, *"The Lord is with you, O valiant warrior...Go in this your strength and deliver Israel...Have I not sent you?"* (Judges 6:12-14)

God, I ask that You totally restore what YOU took not away. The life, health and peace that comes only from You. I pray you protect and defend all that belongs to you Mighty God, their bodies, minds, souls and spirits. God that You restore their vision, clarity and purpose I pray. That Your kingdom come and your will be done in every area of their lives, in the mighty name of Jesus, our Messiah. Amen and Amen.

HEAVEN BUILT FOR ONE?

JUDGING

It seems that we judge ourselves by our good intentions but others by their actions. How fair is that? We condemn others but we want blessings. Why is it that we think we're the only one good enough for heaven, and if that's so, how good would a heaven be with just us? Thank God that His is the better plan. Let's check out our own salvation daily with fear and trembling, as Paul did in *Philippians 2:12*.

Jesus gave HIS view in the Sermon on the Mount:

Do not judge lest you be judged. For in the way you judge, you will be judged; and by your standard of measure, it will be measured to you. And WHY do you look at the speck that is in your brother's eye, but do not notice the log that is in your own eye? Or how can you say to your brother, "Let me take the speck out of your eye," and behold, the log is in your own eye? You hypocrite, first take the log out of your own eye, and then you will see clearly to take the speck out of your brother's eye. (Matthew 7:1-5)

I once had a vision of Judgment Day. God was sitting there with Jesus sitting across from Him and I was getting to watch. A lady came up for her turn.

God asked me, "Barbara, what do you think?"

I said, "God, she was one of the meanest women I've ever known."

The Father looked to the Son and asked, "Son?"

Jesus with tears streaming down His face replied, "Father, You know I came that all might be saved." *(See Luke 9:56)*

At that, God opened the BOOK to see if her name was in it and the vision ended. *(See Revelation 20:11-15)* Well, that's how it is. We may have our opinions but they don't matter at all. God knows everyone's heart and only He can judge righteously.

Paul said, in *1 Corinthians 10:12*, "*therefore let him who thinks he stands, take heed lest he fall.*" The thing to remember is that you've never done anything I couldn't do and I've never done anything you couldn't do. ALL ground is level at the cross. The WORD says, *"ALL* (not y'all) *have sinned,"* Romans 3:23. So, let's just keep our hands and our mouths of everyone else.

It seems the Lord has a list of our proclamations: "I don't, I won't, or I'd never." Watch out, **He is GOD and We are NOT!** I've signed up for many things by judging others when I said, "I'd NEVER," until I learned it's just the grace of God, lest anyone should boast. For we are all made from dust. However, we serve a big God who knows just what it takes to make a keeper out of us and how to make us usable for His kingdom. He said:

"No temptation has overtaken you but such as is common to man; and God is faithful, who will not allow you to be tempted beyond what you are able, but with the temptation will provide the way of escape also, that you may be able to endure it." (1 Corinthians 10:13)

Are you willing to trade places with those you're judging? Remember there's always at least one thing about another man, that only God knows. Job's friends (?) judged and learned.

And it came about after the Lord had spoken these words to Job, that the Lord said to Eliphaz the Temanite, "My wrath is kindled against you and against your two friends, because you have not spoken of Me what is right as My servant Job has. Now therefore, take for yourselves seven bulls and seven rams, and go to My servant Job, and offer up a burnt offering for yourselves, and My servant Job will pray for you. For I will accept him so that I may not do with you according to your folly, because you have not spoken of Me what is right, as My servant Job has." . . . And the Lord accepted Job. And the Lord restored the fortunes of Job when he prayed for his friends, and the Lord increased all that Job had twofold. (Job 42:7-10)

As I counseled a man who felt he was beyond God's forgiveness because of Satan's condemning lies, I had a vision. I saw the spear piercing Jesus' side and as the blood and water gushed out of Him, it turned into a river flowing all over the man, covering him completely with God's cleansing love.

Jesus is ALWAYS there with open arms and **we, the church** must also be doing as He did to the woman at the well in *John 4:7-42.* Our Savior built a bridge TO that woman; he DID NOT

Heaven Built for One?

build a wall that kept her out. The result was, she led the first revival for the King of kings and the Lord of lords.

It's an onward and upward walk for each of us. We can do things today that we'll never have the grace to do tomorrow. God perfects us by turning up the conviction power of the Holy Spirit. He puts His Spirit in us to help us be more like our Savior. Let's set everyone free from our expectations, then:
1. We won't feel bad when they don't live up to them.
2. We'll be blessed by anything nice or thoughtful they do.

It seems, the Pharisees and Sadducees disgusted John the Baptist with their **better than everyone else** attitudes:

You brood of vipers, who warned you to flee from the wrath to come? Therefore bring forth fruit in keeping with repentance; and do not suppose that you can say to yourselves, "We have Abraham for our father," for I say to you, that God is able from these stones to raise up children to Abraham. And the ax is already laid at the root of the trees; every tree therefore that does not bear good fruit is cut down and thrown into the fire.

As for me, I baptize you with water for repentance, but He who is coming after me is mightier than I, and I am not fit to remove His sandals; He will baptize you with the Holy Spirit and fire. And His winnowing fork is in His hand, and He will thoroughly clear His threshing floor, and He will gather His wheat into the barn, but He will burn up the chaff with unquenchable fire. (Matthew 3:7b-12)

That's pretty serious and seems to be a warning to get our OWN house in order. These were the people that thought they had no sin. Jesus went to the sinners because they knew of their need for Him. Remember, the banquet was set, the guests were invited but they chose not to come. So Jesus said to go to the highways and byways and compel them to come in that HIS house may be full. Then He ended the parable of the marriage feast with, *"For many are called, but few are chosen."* (See Matthew 22:1-14) We must choose to be chosen, to work out OUR own salvation with fear and trembling. Remember, all the ground is level at the cross and judge not lest you be judged.

NO SUPERSTARS

Can I Be Your Donkey, Lord?

How many of us knowingly sign up for the DONKEY part of *Numbers 22:22-34?* Let's recount the story of Balaam and his donkey. There was the donkey, just doing his job:

But God was angry because he (Balaam) was going, and the angel of the Lord took his stand in the way as an adversary against him. Now he was riding on his donkey. . . .When the donkey saw the angel of the Lord standing in the way with his drawn sword in his hand, the donkey turned off from the way and went into the field; but Balaam struck the donkey to turn her back into the way. **(First time)**

Then the angel of the Lord stood in a narrow path of the vineyards, with a wall on this side and a wall on that side. When the donkey saw the angel of the Lord, she pressed herself to the wall and pressed Balaam's foot against the wall, so he struck her again. **(Second time)**

And the angel of the Lord went further, and stood in a narrow place where there was no way to turn to the right hand or to the left. When the donkey saw the angel of the Lord, she lay down under Balaam; so Balaam was angry and struck the donkey with his stick. **(Third time)**

And the Lord opened the mouth of the donkey, and she said to Balaam, "What have I done to you, that you have struck me these three times?" Then Balaam said to the donkey, "Because you have made a mockery of me. If there had been a sword in my hand, I would have killed you by now."

NO SUPERSTARS

You can read the rest; but now you know the reward for being a servant, a vessel for the Lord to use. God never said it would be easy; He said that He'd be with us. The praise report of this story is that the DONKEY was USED to save Balaam's life, for only the DONKEY could see the angel with sword drawn to kill her master. Sounds like TOUGH LOVE to me. Sometimes people fight Jesus' servants, those who come in His name, doing as He did. Our Savior warned us in *Matthew 10:24*, "*A disciple is not above his teacher, nor a slave above his master.*"

A synopsis of Paul's view:

For who regards you as superior? And what do you have that you did not receive? But if you did receive it, why do you boast as if you had not received it? You are already filled, you have already become rich, you have become kings without us; and I would indeed that you had become kings so that we also might reign with you.

For, I think, God has exhibited us apostles last of all, as men condemned to death; because we have become a spectacle to the world, both to angels and to men. We are fools for Christ's sake, but you are prudent in Christ; we are weak, but you are strong; you are distinguished, but we are without honor. To this present hour we are both hungry and thirsty, and are poorly clothed, and are roughly treated, and are homeless; and we toil, working with our own hands; when we are reviled, we bless; when we are persecuted, we endure; when we are slandered, we try to conciliate; we have become as the scum of the world, the dregs of all things, even until now. (1 Corinthians 4:7-13)

Well, how about it, are YOU ready to follow that Galilean with the nail-scarred hands? To go where He sends, to say what He says, and to do what He wants you to do? Paul was ready to follow wherever He led which was why he could also say:

But I will come to you soon, if the Lord wills, and I shall find out, not the words of those who are arrogant, but their power. For the kingdom of God does not consist in words, but in power. (1 Corinthians 4:19-20)

Will we put down all that we are to become as nothing? That's exactly what God hangs the sun, moon and stars on, NOTHING. So let's walk with nothing to protect or defend above our walk with Him so He can use us too. To die to all that we are so that He can live through us.

The last days army is going to be made up of the NOBODIES from NOWHERE that don't care what the SOMEBODIES from SOMEWHERE have to say! Pride is a monster that eats up the God in us. You can leave the past behind when you repent. Then you're forgiven and can go forth. (Luke 24:47) No past: to regret, complain about, or to brag about. ALL must glorify God.

Paul said, *"Forgetting what lies behind and reaching forward to what lies ahead. I press on toward the goal for the prize of the upward call of God in Christ Jesus." (Philippians 3:13-14)*

Is your testimony bringing praise to you or to God? Is it, "I can do all things," or is it, *"I can do ALL things through Christ Who strengthens me?" (Philippians 4:13)*

It seems there's a door that leads into usefulness for Christ that's only big enough for you alone to fit through. You have to leave all that you have, and are, behind. Nothing goes through with you. However, on the other side, God has lots of presents.

Will we be faceless ministers of the gospel of Jesus Christ, drawing no attention to ourselves?

In his book, My Utmost for His Highest, Oswald Chambers explains the Lord's call to him, **"I reckon on you for extreme service with no complaining on your part and no explanation on mine."**

That rather sums it all up. Moment by moment, to give that crown back to Jesus, for His honor and glory. Knowing that without HIM we are nothing and can do nothing. You see, if we think God can't do it without us, our pride and arrogance may get us benched from further duty. May we never take the glory but give it to Him. The Lord said in *Isaiah 46:4b, "I have done it, and I shall carry you; and I shall bear you, and I shall deliver you."*

NO SUPERSTARS

God does it. **GOD IS GOD and We are NOT!** What is permissible for an ordinary man or woman just isn't for a man or woman called by the sovereignty of God to be used for His honor and glory. Others may - you cannot. Will we be a KEEPER? *(See Matthew 13:3-52)* The desire to get credit for what God is doing through you will get you out of the flow of the Holy Spirit. It's enough that God knows. Beyond that it's your little secret. Don't tell. It's your great adventure with God. ENJOY IT.

Once the Lord sent Nick and me to the Hospital with the assignment to pray for the kids at 3 p.m. However, when we arrived, there was a big sign posted in the children's wing, "No visiting allowed, REST TIME for the children."

"But God, You said to be here at 3:00."

"Yes, I did. There'll be no laying on of hands, that way, I'LL be sure to get ALL the glory."

We sat on the bench OUTSIDE the children's wing to intercede for each of the children God brought before us in prayer. We left feeling there was one more child, with muscular dystrophy, that needed prayer. As we were going out the Emergency Room exit, the paramedics were unloading a child in a wheelchair from an ambulance who had muscular dystrophy.

God knows EVERYTHING and lets us know what we need to know to be USED by Him. Speaking of being USED, when you got saved, did you ever say something like, "God, use me?" Well, do you ever feel USED? Hallelujah, God Almighty is answering your prayers. Praise HIM. Also, remember we must always be free enough to give, and humble enough to receive.

We should never brag on our own accomplishments for we have nothing that God didn't give us. That breath we're breathing, those shoes on our feet, our bodies that work, they are ALL from God. Have we thanked HIM today?

We can give out His love, compassion, and tenderness to a hurt and dying world that doesn't care who we are or what we've done. It's all about one beggar telling another beggar where the free bread is so he can live. Will we be poured-out wine and broken bread for a lost and dying world today? People don't care how much we know until they know how much we care.

Jesus said:

> Then the King will answer and say to them, "Truly I say to you, to the extent that you did it to one of these brothers of Mine, even the least of them, you did it to Me," Matthew 25:45.

The question is, ARE WE? Are we doing it to the least of them in His name? Or are we loving ourselves by pampering our flesh with its wants and desires, caring nothing for HIS kingdom? Someday that answer will be all that matters. Read *Matthew 25:31-46* to get God's view concerning heaven or hell.

> Paul said, "To the weak I became weak, that I might win the weak; I have become all things to all men, that I may by all means save some. And I do all things for the sake of the gospel, that I may become a fellow partaker of it. . . .Therefore, I run in such a way, as not without aim; I box in such a way, as not beating the air; but I buffet my body and make it my slave, lest possibly, after I have preached to others, I myself should be disqualified."
> (1 Corinthians 9:22-23, 26-27)

Paul's only boast was in the cross of Christ. We should go and do likewise. Jesus said, "GO and DO." *James 1:22* says to *"be DOERS of the Word and not merely hearer's only.*

CHAINED TO THINGS?

Leave it all and follow ME

(Or...How to Hear the Voice of God)

Hearing God's voice. Now that's a real challenge because we become a disciple of who we listen to, and whatever we take in. Who is lord of our ears, eyes, mouth, mind, body, and finances? How do you know God's voice? Can't you tell your mother's voice from all the others? God's voice is also very distinct, just like your mom's. How do you hear God? You shut out all the other voices; the television, newspapers, radio, telephones. Everyone is listening to some voice. What we hear should line up with the Bible, the Word of God.

Jesus said, "Take heed how you hear." (Luke 8:18)

God will let you know anything you need to know to walk in the realm He's called you to walk. We waste precious time from the call of God on our lives. We get into business that's not ours by taking on the clutter and confusion of others when we have no authority to deal with it

Make it your ambition to lead a quiet life and attend to your own business and work with your hands.
(1 Thessalonians 4:11)

When God was calling me to that higher place of abode with Him, He had me get rid of the TV, all the books, tapes, magazines, newspapers and other clutter. He said, "It's Holy Ghost and knees time. Read the Word. You don't have time to waste on the distractions of other people's lives. You are the only you I have. Stay in My Word and on your knees and I will speak to you. Moses did and heard My voice, so shall you. Then you'll go out and do what I've called you to do, empowered by ME, hearing MY voice, and doing what I say. There's just not time left for regurgitated knowledge."

As for you, the anointing which you received from Him abides in you, and you have no need for anyone to teach you; but as His anointing teaches you about all things, and is true and is not a lie, and just as it has taught you, you abide in Him. (1 John 2:27)

Pick God over EVERYTHING - for one day we shall give account for every minute, every dollar, and every word. Oh God, in Your grace and mercy forgive us for all the time, money, and energy we've squandered and *"redeem the time, for the days are evil." (Ephesians 5:16)*

OK guys, this is your paragraph - about that television, or should I call it the hellevision? How is it that you can yell, scream, and jump up and down for a pigskin and not for God? Only God is worthy of ALL praise and if He is your God, then BOW. If that TV is your god then at least be honest and bow down to it. Do you know as much about the Bible and its ways as you do those sports figures and their ways? It's a question of priorities and all eternity awaits your decision. One day there will be an accounting for the time God has given us and how we have invested it.

Love not the world, nor the things in the world. If anyone loves the world, the love of the Father is not in him. For all that is in the world, the lust of the flesh and the lust of the eyes and the boastful pride of life, is not from the Father, but is from the world. And the world is passing away, and also its lusts; but the one who does the will of God abides forever. (1 John 2:15-17)

It's time to get your house in order and go free. Whether it's to sell it, give it away, or throw it out. Let's get rid of the junk in our lives.

Jesus said, "NO ONE of you can be My disciple who does not give up all his own possessions." (Luke 14:33)

When the Lord told me to leave it all and follow Him, He instructed me to invite a single mother in the church to come and get whatever she wanted for a fresh new beginning. She

Chained to Things?

did, and when all her new furniture was delivered and in place, she sat down and started crying. I asked her what was wrong? She replied, "Every time I sat down on that old sofa I'd remember being thrown down on it." She'd been a victim of abuse and God was healing her by giving her all new furniture for her new beginning. Then she could pass on her old stuff to someone else. She was blessed to be a blessing.

After Nick died, God told me to get his stuff out of the house. Let go of the past and begin again. The graveyard is no place for a child of God.

Jesus said, "Follow Me. . . .Allow the dead to bury their own dead; but as for you, go and proclaim everywhere the kingdom of God. . . . No one, after putting his hand to the plow and looking back, is fit for the kingdom of God." (Luke 9:59-62)

Let the dead bury the dead? There's death back there, let them bury each other. But YOU come on...when you hear Him calling you to "Come." It's a choice we all have. Choose LIFE. There's nothing we can do about the past but repent, forgive and then let it go.

Paul said, "One thing I do, forgetting what lies behind and reaching forward to what lies ahead, I press on toward the goal for the prize of the upward call of God in Christ Jesus." (Philippians 3:13b-14)

We MUST go forward. God put no rear-view mirrors on our heads and our eyes are in front, aimed forward, as we should be. *Isaiah 43:18-21* speaks so clearly:

DON'T look back, or ponder the things of the past. Behold I make ALL things new. . . .I make roadways in the wilderness and streams in the desert. . . .So you will praise ME.

Will we? Will we throw away those shovels and quit digging up old graves, to go forth? We have a choice today. God always said, *"IF."* Jesus always said, *"IF any man would come."*

So must we. Everyone has a choice to receive or to reject not only God, but also the God in you. However, the Lord will call for showdowns as Elijah did on Mount Carmel:

> *How long will you hesitate between two opinions? If the Lord is God, follow Him; but if Baal, follow him.* (1 Kings 18:21)

Joshua reiterated that same choice as they entered the Promised Land…

> *Choose for yourselves today whom you will serve. . . but as for me and my house, we will serve the Lord.* (Joshua 24:15)

It's a decision we all have to make individually. However, the standard is, when you are rejected because of the God you serve - bless them and pray for God in His mercy to send someone else to warn them or minister to them. Because hell is a hot place fit only for Satan and his demons. God's heart is that none perish. However, He will not always strive with man.

> *Today, if you hear His voice, do not harden your hearts, as when they provoked Me. . . .As I swore in My wrath they shall not enter My rest. . . .They were not able to enter because of unbelief. Therefore, let us fear lest, while a promise remains of entering His rest, any one of you should seem to have come short of it.* (Hebrews 3:7b-4:1)

> *The fear of the Lord is the beginning of wisdom.* (Psalm 111:10)

Today is that promised day of rest for all who will, to come. Go through the dying to get free from all the entanglements of life. For if you're not free to do what God has called you to do, you're BOUND, and that's no way for a child of God to live. Pay the price to go free and to owe no man anything but the love of Jesus Christ. That way, *"if they don't receive you, kick the dust off your feet and walk on."* Read *Matthew 10*, it's a great chapter. It's Jesus' impartation to His disciples.

Even though none go with me, I'll follow Him. Wherever He leads, I'll go. Ask God to give you His next course of events for your life. However, before you expect an answer to that prayer, be sure YOUR house is in order. If it's not, repent for slothfulness and laziness. Do what you know you should and THEN you'll get the next piece, the next course of events for

Chained to Things?

your life. God will not add to a mess of clutter, confusion, and unfinished business. It's important to get the old cleared out to make way for the NEW.

God told Ezekiel, *"Even though these three men, Noah, Daniel, and Job were in its midst, by their own righteousness they could only deliver themselves." (Ezekiel 14:14,16,18, and 20)*

That's just how it is. Jesus Christ had to say,

"Who is My mother and who are My brothers?" And stretching out His hand toward His disciples, He said, "Behold, My mother and My brothers. For whoever does the will of My Father who is in heaven, he is My brother and sister and mother." (Matthew 12:48-50)

Jesus knew the cost. It costs EVERYTHING. A man told a great pianist, "I'd give my life to play as you do." To which the pianist replied, "I DID."

Jim Elliot, the missionary, who gave his life for the cause of Christ in Equador in 1956 said, "He is no fool, who gives what he cannot keep to gain what he cannot lose." Peter also warns us:

> *For speaking out arrogant words of vanity they entice by fleshly desires, by sensuality, those who barely escape from the ones who live in error, promising them freedom while they themselves are slaves of corruption; for by what a man is overcome, by this he is enslaved. For if after they have escaped the defilement of the world by the knowledge of the Lord and Savior Jesus Christ, they are again entangled in them and are overcome, the last state has become worse for them than the first. For it would be better for them not to have known the way of righteousness, than having known it, to turn away from the holy commandment delivered to them. It has happened to them according to the true proverb, "A dog returns to its own vomit," and, "A sow after washing, returns to wallowing in the mire." (2 Peter 2:18-22)*

Is that what we want? Brothers and sisters, we have to pay the price to go onward and upward for the cause of Christ. We just don't know how many days, months, or years we have to make a difference. Trust God to take you into HIS very best plan for your life, free of distractions, where you hear the voice of the living God. Remember that doubts and fears will steal your dreams and visions. However, when you are in the center of God's will, where He has called you for that time and season, there is perfect protection and peace. I pray that God in His love and mercy will keep you on fertile field where His Spirit is moving.

The Lord is preparing to pour out His Spirit upon His servants for this last-day battle call. He is not into validating our plans. The Holy Spirit blows where it will, and **GOD IS GOD** and free to change our lives at HIS discretion.

No soldier in active service entangles himself in the affairs of everyday life, so that he may please the one who enlisted him as a soldier. (2 Timothy 2:4)

You are not our own--for you have been bought with a price: therefore glorify God in your body. (1 Corinthians 6:19-20)

Don't try to put flesh clothes on spiritual things or to clothe the Spirit with flesh, it just won't work. God is holy and His ways are perfect.

Truly, truly, I say to you, unless one is born of the water and the Spirit, he cannot enter into the kingdom of God. That which is born of the flesh is flesh, and that which is born of the Spirit is spirit. Do not marvel that I said to you, "You must be born again." The wind blows where it wishes and you hear the sound of it, but do not know where it comes from and where it is going; so is everyone who is born of the Spirit. (John 3:5-8)

JESUS SAID THAT. Have you been born again? Born of the Spirit? Today is your day….Just say "Yes" to Jesus. Ask Him to come into your heart, forgive you of your sins and change your life. He likes prayers like that…they work!

THE CHRISTMAS ISSUE

The game is over when SOMEONE quits playing

Christmas. The birth of Jesus Christ!

Easter. Resurrection Day. The day our Lord rose from the dead!

Reasons to rejoice in the Lord.

Church, let's not let the world come in and steal the sacredness of these days. THESE are the things to impart to our children.

THE TRUTH
Jesus, in the manger is what Christmas is about.
Jesus, risen from the dead is what Easter is about.

Let's remember what the real meaning of Christmas is and appreciate the gift God gave. The greatest gift of all. Who did Santa Claus die for? Who can he save from hell? Does anyone care that God came as a child, so man could have communion with his Maker once again? Let's be thankful for all the gifts God has given, especially Jesus. Let's focus on the change and salvation that one little baby boy brought into the world - what He saved you from and what He entitles you to have. He covered your past, takes care of your present and purchased your forever. What a gift!

Easter is all about that baby, now a man, hanging on the cross to pay for our sins. After being in the grave three days, the stone was rolled away and our Savior came forth, victorious over death, hell and the grave. He paid the price so we could have access to our heavenly Father, be forgiven by the power of His blood, healed by His stripes…victorious over every enemy of our lives, souls and calls.

A question…If you raise your children lying to them about that Santa character and the Easter Bunny (who they CAN see)…WHY should they believe you when you try (after you've been exposed) to untangle this mess and tell them about the Savior, Jesus Christ (who they CAN'T see) and about the REAL meaning of both Christmas and Easter? We are charged by one of the Ten Commandments *(Exodus 20:1-17)* not to lie.

James 5:12 admonishes, "Let your yes be yes, and your no, no; so that you may not fall under judgment."

Jesus said in Matthew 12:34-37: *"And I say to you, that every careless word that men shall speak, they shall render account for it in the day of judgment. For by your words you shall be justified, and by your words you shall be condemned."*

Who are we lifting up by this "fairy tale?" Jesus said, *"If I be lifted up, I will draw all men to Myself." (John 12:32)*

We're lifting up someone at Christmas-time, and it should be our blessed Savior. In my own life the day came when I smashed all those little Santa Clauses. Yes, even the BIG ceramic one Mother made with her own hands.

As a Christian business-woman, I'd always run a

Happy Birthday, Jesus

ad on Christmas morning. However, this was a different year. God was delivering me of all distortion, no matter what the area. There's only truth and there's only lie.

This particular Christmas, the ad was

The Christmas Issue

Guess who the irate calls were from? Offended Christians asking, "How can you put that in the paper? What if my children had seen it?"

"By the time your child read to page 5 of The Arkansas Democrat, they would have read about all kinds of garbage - so for someone to finally tell them the truth – you should REJOICE." Remember that any game is over when someone quits playing and the Body of Christ IS going free. Call that radical? That's probably what the religious leaders of Jesus' day called HIM, radical. He also threw the moneychangers out of the temple and believed in truth and honesty. But free is free. Jesus Christ is my Lord, Savior, and King; to HIM and HIM only shall I bow. Don't you bend down to put those presents under that tree? It was God, who said:

> For the customs of the peoples are delusion; because it is wood cut from the forest, the work of the hands of a craftsman with a cutting tool. They decorate it with silver and with gold; they fasten it with nails and with hammers, so that it will not totter. (Jeremiah 10:3-4)

Christmas trees? Idolatry? Delusion? Church, let's get delivered and go free – for the game truly is over when SOMEONE quits playing – and NO ONE can make you play stupid games.

That same Christmas I went to K-Mart to buy a Nativity Book for my Sunday School class. There was NOT ONE to be found, instead the racks were overflowing with "those others"....the Santa Books.

Now Christians, before you get offended at my way of touching this issue, how about, in the privacy of your own home, answering the following three questions:

1. Did you spend money that you didn't have this Christmas?
2. Did you spend time that you didn't have WHILE spending money you didn't have this Christmas?
3. Did playing this game take you out of the peace and the presence of God in ANY way?

It's a game...that's over when someone quits playing. To test this word; see how many people continue bestowing gifts upon you AFTER you quit playing the game. Go ahead, test it. Wasn't it just a flesh, payback game? It was just a game, but Jesus came to "set the captives FREE."

So, church, let's get FREE from these myths and fables

> *But now that you have come to know God, or rather to be known by God, how is it that you turn back again to the weak and worthless elemental things, to which you desire to be enslaved all over again? (Galatians 4:9)*
>
> *But have nothing to do with worldly fables fit only for old women. On the other hand, discipline yourself for the purpose of godliness. (1 Timothy 4:7)*
>
> *Nor pay attention to myths and endless genealogies, which give rise to mere speculation rather than furthering the administration of God which is by faith. But the goal of our instruction is love from a pure heart and a good conscience and a sincere faith. (1 Timothy 1:4-5)*

There are so many other things to do with our time, energy, and money that will be of eternal value when we come face to face with Jesus Christ. Let's be consumed with HIS call, HIS purpose, and HIS glory while we are on this earth for that's ALL that's going to last. Hallelujah. BE FREE.

Fear of man or people pleasing will keep you bound.
Please read the following scriptures:

Job 32:21-22, Proverbs 29:25, Isaiah 51:7,12-13,57:11, Daniel 3:15-18, John 12:42-43, Galatians 1:10, Ephesians 6:6-7, Hebrews 13:6, and Jude 16.

LET'S GET SAVED CHURCH
and GO...Do the Stuff

The greatest miracle is when someone is born-again into the kingdom of God. Saving souls is why we're here. There should be healings and all forms of miracles; but that's just a part of the walk. The real reason we're here is to lead people to Jesus. Some reply, "I go to church."

"Well, that's nice, but are you saved?" Many people go to church. Do you KNOW JESUS as your PERSONAL Savior? Do you walk with Him and talk with Him? Is HE your best friend? It all starts when you ask Jesus into your heart.

Jesus said, "I am the way, and the truth, and the life; no one comes to the Father, but through Me." (John 14:6)

"For all have sinned and fall short of the glory of God." (Romans 3:23)

"For the wages of sin is death, but the free gift of God is eternal life in Christ Jesus our Lord." (Romans 6:23)

"But God demonstrates His own love toward us, in that while we were yet sinners, Christ died for us." (Romans 5:8)

"Repent therefore and return, that your sins may be wiped away, in order that times of refreshing may come from the presence of the Lord." (Acts 3:19)

"If you confess with your mouth Jesus as Lord, and believe in your heart that God raised Him from the dead, you shall be saved. . . .for whoever will call upon the name of the Lord shall be saved." (Romans 10:9,13)

Jesus said, "For God so loved the world, that He gave His only begotten Son, that whoever believes in Him should not perish, but have eternal life." (John 3:16)

For by grace you have been saved through faith; and that not of yourselves, it is the gift of God; not as a result of works, that no one should boast. (Ephesians 2:8)

Jesus said, "I am the door, if anyone enters through Me, he shall be saved. . . .the thief comes only to steal, and kill, and destroy; I came that they might have life, and might have it abundantly. I am the good shepherd; the *good shepherd lays down His life for the sheep." (John 10:9-11)*

If you've never asked Jesus to come into your life as Lord and Savior, I ask you to settle that issue now by praying this prayer:

Heavenly Father, Thank You for sending Jesus. I believe He is Your Son and that He died on the cross for me. Jesus, I ask You to come into my heart and forgive me for all my sins, cleanse me, change me and make me a new person. Show me Your will for my life and give me the strength to do it, for now I receive You as my personal Savior and I pray this prayer in Jesus name.

Saving souls must be a normal occurrence for us, for if a person is lost, they're going to hell and if we know the truth and don't do anything about it, we stand guilty. Jesus died for sinners so we must go forth and tell them about His love. That's the good news. One night during the ministry time, a young man came up for prayer. He told me that he'd had a very good friend, who had started hanging out with the wrong crowd. He had gotten busy and never checked up on the friend, and one day the call came that he had overdosed on drugs and died. Now, when this man tried to sleep, he had nightmares of this friend (?) screaming out from hell, "Why didn't you tell me...I thought you were my friend...and now, it's too late.

Here's the gospel on that issue. Please read it. Jesus spells out very clearly what we are called to DO if we are His:

He gave them authority over unclean spirits, to cast them out, and to heal every kind of disease and every kind of sickness. . . .These twelve Jesus sent out after instructing them, saying, ". . .Go to the lost sheep of the house of Israel. And as you go, preach, saying, 'The kingdom of heaven is at hand.' Heal the sick, raise the dead, cleanse the lepers, cast out demons; freely you received, freely give." (Matthew 10:1,5-8)

Isn't that rather clear? GO AND DO. PERIOD. So, the first order of business is usually to quit playing church and get saved for real. Then give your life, body, mind, soul and spirit to God through the atonement of His Son, Jesus Christ. Repent for your sins, be forgiven, and change. Get free to go do the stuff He's called you to do. SIMPLE. However, I must in all honesty tell you that it WILL cost you your LIFE. Everything that doesn't look like Jesus will get burned up, BUT you'll be FREE. Hallelujah, because we're not going to take any of this stuff with us anyway. Church is not to be a spectator sport. Rather it is to be a place where every child of God is before the throne worshipping Him individually.

We've got to get back to doing the basics better (reading the Bible, praying, giving, etc.) for it takes all parts of the Christian walk to stay healthy. The Dead Sea is dead, because it just takes in and doesn't give out, so it has become the most polluted body of water in the world. Take a hint from the Dead Sea. We GET to give. *"Freely we have received, freely, we give."* (Matthew 10:8) It keeps us in shape, and keeps us from becoming fat babies that just take in, have our diapers changed, and are cared for. Church, it's time to grow up and go make disciples. Jesus' great commission to ALL of us is:

> *All authority has been given to Me in heaven and on earth. GO therefore and make disciples of all the nations, baptizing them in the name of the Father and the Son and the Holy Spirit, teaching them to observe all that I commanded you; and lo, I am with you always, even to the end of the age. (Matthew 28:18-20)*

We must ask ourselves, "Am I about the Father's business, doing the stuff, or am I just playing religious games?" Peter was a mess before Pentecost, but afterward he was on fire for God and mightily anointed. The Holy Ghost made the difference. So please, don't sit in your dead church thinking you have all you need. If you have the goods you ARE filled with the Holy Ghost. If not, you NEED to be. For dead is dead and alive is alive. It's just that until we know there's more, we think we have it.

One thing that drew me in was the LIFE that the alive folks were speaking and ministering. People were living - not just going home being the same mess to the same mess. Lives were being changed. And 2,000 years later, Jesus is still touching lives through His Spirit-filled and sanctified children, who have paid the price to die to dead religion, the *"tradition of* the elders that makes the Word of God of no effect," (Mark 7:3-13) and to what religious people think. The blind man was thrown out of the synagogue in *John 9* AFTER Jesus opened his eyes; for speaking a simple statement of truth:

> "Well, here is an amazing thing, that you do not know where He is from, and yet He opened my eyes. We know that God does not hear sinners, but if anyone is God-fearing, and does His will, He hears him. Since the beginning of time it has never been heard that anyone opened the eyes of a person born blind. If this man were not from God, He could do nothing." They answered and said to him, "You were born entirely in sin, and are you teaching us?" And they put him out.

That's still happening today. If you don't have IT (the Holy Spirit), pray to get it. Be willing to have your spirit opened to receive all that Jesus left for you. Hungry people don't care who feed them; they just want to eat. It's okay to be needy.

> Jesus said, "Blessed are the poor in spirit, for theirs is the kingdom of heaven." (Matthew 5:3)

Poor in the spirit is when you want and need more of God than you have. He also said:

> Ask and it shall be given to you; seek, and you shall find; knock, and it shall be opened to you. . . .If you then, being evil, know how to give good gifts to your children, how much more shall your heavenly Father give the Holy Spirit to those who ask Him? (Luke 11:9-13)

Jesus left us here to do the work to prepare for His return. He's sitting at the Father's right hand and we are to be His arms, legs, feet, and mouth. We are HIS body. If all Christians were like you, would the world be saved? It seems futile to argue over Greek and Hebrew word studies, and men's varied interpretations, when the big question is - are you living in obedience to everything you know the WORD says to do? Are you doing the "go ye's," or are you fighting over words which will profit nothing to your account when you meet Jesus face to face? It's too late to be singing three songs, hearing a message, and going home unchanged. We have so many

Let's Get Saved, Church

spiritually aborted and stillborn in the church that we're powerless to go to the nations with the good news. This is a wake-up call. The Church is YOU and the Church is ME. God said in *James 1:22-27, "Prove yourselves doers of the Word, and not merely hearers who delude themselves."*

So the question is, "Do those books and tapes that you're taking in lead you to DOING?" You could start by telling everyone you meet, "Jesus loves you." Everyone wants love, it's just that so many are looking for it in all the wrong places because we've never told them where He is...love...that is.

Jesus loves you, this I know, for the Bible tells me so!

Jesus said, "GO" and obedience is always the dividing issue. Start where you are but DO something for Jesus today. Jesus is still the great potter looking for unlikely pieces of clay to use. Will you be used today? "Jesus, is that you in there?" We as Christians all carry a piece of Jesus. I need your piece and you need mine.

One word of warning: hurt people - hurt people. Don't be afraid of those hurt brothers and sisters. Instead love them and pray for them. Ministry is meeting needs and healing hurts. Jesus is still fixing and healing today, just as He was 2,000 years ago, and calls us to go and do likewise. He said in *John 14:12:*

> *Truly, truly, I say to you, he who believes in Me, the works that I do shall he do also; and GREATER works than these shall he do; because I go to the Father.*

Are we doing those greater works He spoke of? The Church of Jesus Christ should be taking up where He left off.

> *And He said to them, "Go into all the world and preach the gospel to ALL creation. He who has believed and has been baptized shall be saved; but he who has disbelieved shall be condemned. And these signs shall accompany those who have believed: in My name they will cast out demons, they will speak with new tongues; they will pick up serpents, and if they drink any deadly poison, it shall not hurt them; they will lay hands on the sick, and they will recover."*

> So then, when the Lord Jesus had spoken to them, He was received up into heaven, and sat down at the right hand of God. And they went out and preached everywhere while the Lord worked with them and confirmed the Word by the SIGNS that followed. (Mark 16:15-20)

Jesus leaves no room for doubt or discussion on that issue. If you're not doing what He called you to do, STOP whatever you're doing, check out your salvation, then get filled with the Holy Spirit and GO and DO whatever your Master commands:
> "Be ye DOERS of the WORD."

Being filled with the Holy Spirit is an important step for every believer. Receiving the Holy Spirit is evidenced by speaking in tongues in the Bible. Concerning the day of Pentecost:
> And there appeared to them tongues as of fire distributing themselves, and they rested on each one of them. And they were ALL filled with the Holy Spirit and began to speak with other TONGUES, as the Spirit was giving them utterance. (Acts 2:3-4)

This is not my view or interpretation, it is what the BIBLE says. That experience turned Peter from a mess who had denied Christ into an anointed man of God who could then say:
> "I do not possess silver and gold, but what I do have, I give to you: In the Name of Jesus Christ, the Nazarene--WALK." (Acts 3:6) And the man did.

Peter shared how the Gentiles received the Holy Spirit:
> While Peter was still speaking these words, the Holy Spirit fell upon all those who were listening to the message. And all the circumcised believers who had come with Peter were amazed, because the gift of the Holy Spirit had been poured out upon the Gentiles also. For they were hearing them speaking with TONGUES and exalting God. (Acts 10:44-46)

Also, when Paul went to Ephesus and found some disciples:
> And said to them, "Did you receive the Holy Spirit when you believed?" And they said to him, "No, we have not even heard whether there is a Holy Spirit.". . . And Paul said, "John baptized with the baptism of repentance,

telling the people to believe in Him who was coming after him, that is, in Jesus." And when they heard this, they were baptized in the name of the Lord Jesus. And when Paul had laid his hands upon them, the Holy Spirit came on them, and they began speaking with TONGUES and prophesying. (Acts 19:2-6)
Paul's first indication that they weren't filled with the Holy Spirit was that they had no power.

Holding to a form of godliness, although they have denied its power, and avoid such men as these. (2Timothy 3:5)
It's sort of like spending $100,000 on the top of the line Mercedes and not getting an engine. Who would stand for that? But sadly enough, many churches are telling people that this gift isn't for today. That, my friends, is letting the tradition of the elders make the Word of God of no effect. What a lie, to steal from God's kids the very power Jesus promised. (Read John 14-17) Wake up church! Don't stand for that anymore; time is running out. Be filled with the Holy Spirit.

And in the same way, the Spirit also helps our weakness; for we do not know how to pray as we should, but the Spirit Himself intercedes for us with groanings too deep for words; and He who searches the hearts knows what the mind of the Spirit is, because He intercedes for the saints according to the will of God. (Romans 8:26-27)
God makes His views very clear so let's quit fighting what GOD has ordained, for we will not win. **GOD IS GOD and We are NOT!** Be normal. It's normal to be filled with the Spirit, talk in tongues, and praise God. Speaking in tongues is a heavenly prayer language that confounds your intellect and allows you direct access to the heart of the Father.

If you don't like loving and praising Him on this side, you probably won't like heaven either. However, aren't we all praising someone or something most of the time? Check it out by taping some of your conversations. Or, to find out who your god really is, take a look at your checkbook. Let's get delivered of materialism and idolatry. Get filled with the Holy Ghost and sign up for the journey of a lifetime, never again returning to old dead religion.

Go where God sends.

Do what He says to do.
Say what He says.
THAT is normal for a child of God.

Let's rise up and do something that's going to matter, for only what's done for God will last.

When I had three stores, and ten on the drawing board, God asked, "Barbara, when are you going to do something for ME?" Well, brothers and sisters, God in His love and mercy knows how to burn out all our idols, and with them go what people think, the fear of man, and the respect of people that we find we've been bowing to - the voices rather than THE VOICE.

We have been approved by God to be entrusted with the gospel, so we speak, not as pleasing men but God, who examines our hearts. For we never came with flattering speech, as you know, nor with a pretext for greed--God is witness--nor did we seek glory from men, either from you or from others. (1Thessalonians 2:4-6)

How can you believe, when you receive glory from one another, and you do not seek the glory that is from the one and only God? (John 5:44)

You were bought with a price; do not become slaves of men. (1 Corinthians 7:23)

I, even I, am He who comforts you. Who are you that you are afraid of man who dies, and the son of man who is made like grass; that you have forgotten the Lord your Maker, who stretched out the heavens, and laid the foundations of the earth; that you fear continually all day long because of the fury of the oppressor, as he makes ready to destroy?

But where is the fury of the oppressor? The exile will soon be set free, and will not die in the dungeon, nor will his bread be lacking. For I am the Lord your God, who stirs up the sea and its waves roar (the Lord of hosts is His name). And I have put My words in your mouth, and have covered you with the shadow of My hand, to establish the heavens, to found the earth, and to say to Zion, "You are My people." (Isaiah 51:12-16)

God, forgive us and cleanse us of the defilement of the world. Jesus had to say to Peter,

> *Get behind Me Satan. You are a stumbling block to Me; for you are not setting your mind on God's interests, but man's. (Matthew 16:23)*

Sometimes, it's the people who love us most that would abort the call of God on our lives. My family's love would never have allowed me to go through what I HAD to go through to be free. So I guess it was a good thing that I was disowned for leaving all to follow Jesus. It seems no one can go with us through the dying. We must go through alone with God as He turns up the fire. Rather than whine and complain, it seems we should admit that much of what we're going through we signed up for ourselves through our rebellion to God and His laws. For isn't free will actually rebellion to God?

Oh Lord, don't give me any choices. I'd just rather be a clone of Yours so I don't miss You. I desire above all to go where you send, to do what You say do, and to say what You say.

You see Saul consulted a witch BECAUSE the Spirit of God had departed from him. *(See 1 Samuel 28)* We, also, get to choose. Guard your heart.

> *See to it that no one comes short of the grace of God; that no root of bitterness springing up causes trouble, and by it many be defiled. (Hebrews 12:15)*

Forgive and you will be forgiven.

> *For if you forgive men for their transgressions, your heavenly Father will also forgive you. But if you do not forgive men, then your Father will not forgive your transgressions. (Matthew 6:14-15)*

Trust God and wait on His answer. WAIT seems to be one of the hardest words in the English language.

> *Yet those who wait for the Lord will gain new strength; they will mount up with wings like eagles, they will run and not get tired, they will walk and not become weary. (Isaiah 40:31)*

When you've done all - STAND. Satan drives but the Holy Spirit guides. If you are being driven, know that it is NOT God.

I pray that God will:

> *Bring you into a broad place; that He will rescue you, because He delights in you. . .that He will make your way*

blameless...that He make your feet like hinds' feet, and set you upon your high places." (Psalm 18)

I ask the Lord to give you a fresh vision and purpose for all He's called you into.

For without a vision, the people perish. (Proverbs 29:18)

I come against all death, defilement, discouragement and disease in your life. LIVE in Jesus name. I ask God to fill you with his Holy Spirit and give you an expectancy for the future with the hope to go on, from the very throne of God. That *He put before you an open door that no man can shut,* for opportunity and new beginnings, *and that He shut those doors no man can open,* for your protection. *(Revelation 3:7-8)* I ask God to keep you on fertile field, where His blessing is.

I pray that He draw the line and call for a showdown with all the forces coming against you, and win every battle on your behalf in Jesus name. Amen and AMEN. *(See 1 Samuel 16 and 2 Chronicles 20.)*

Many times God has to take the chalkboard of our lives and either break it, or erase it, to give us a new chalkboard written on by the hand of the living God *(Daniel 5).* His will done HIS way.

So many things just don't make the cut in our Christian lives. It seems the closer we get to God, His fire of holiness, purity and Christ-likeness burns them out. Hallelujah, let them go. Keep walking, man or woman of God, and do what your hands find to do. The quicker we do what's before us, the quicker we get the next step. Pray each morning, "Lord, what would You like me to do today?" Desire above all that each step of the way be guided by His still small voice. Remember that it was AFTER the strong wind, AFTER the earthquake, and AFTER the fire that the voice of God came to Elijah. *(1 Kings 19)* Concerning that unshaken kingdom:

And His voice shook the earth then, but now He has promised, saying, "YET ONCE MORE I WILL SHAKE NOT ONLY THE EARTH, BUT ALSO THE HEAVEN." And this expression, "Yet once more" denotes the removing of those things which can be shaken, as of created things, in order that those things which cannot be shaken may remain. Therefore, since we receive a kingdom which cannot be shaken, let us show gratitude, by which we may offer to God an acceptable service with reverence and awe, for our God is a consuming fire. (Hebrews 12:26-29)

However, after the winds, after the shaking, and after everything being burned up, then to hear the voice of the living GOD... makes it worth the trip.

I tell all clutter, confusion and distractions to leave you in Jesus' name. I ask God to give you the next course of events for your life - the path that leads to life and not death. That He takes you into His peace and presence where there's life to live and life to give. God never said it would be easy. He said, *"I'll be with you."* So shake off those grave clothes and march forward child of the Most High God, it's onward and upward from here. *(See Isaiah 51:22-52:2.)*

ONE DAY, Joseph left his dungeon:

Then Pharaoh sent and called for Joseph, and they HURRIEDLY brought him out of the dungeon; and when he had shaved himself and changed his clothes, he came to Pharaoh. THEN, Pharaoh said to his servants, "Can we find a man like this, in whom is a divine spirit?" So Pharaoh said to Joseph, "Since God has informed you of all this, there is no one so discerning and wise as you are. You shall be over my house, and according to your command all my people shall do homage; only in the throne I will be greater than you."...And he set him over ALL the land of Egypt." (Genesis 41:14-43)

Now that's a promotion. Another ONE DAY that's significant is that of Jehoiachin, king of Judah in *Jeremiah 52:32-33:*

Then he spoke kindly to him and set his throne above the thrones of the kings who were with him in Babylon. So Jehoiachin changed his prison clothes, and had his meals in the king's presence regularly all the days of his life.

Promotions from the hand of God are the only ones that will stand, for it is God who humbles the proud and who lifts up the lowly. *(See Daniel 4).* One day, SUDDENLY things change. You may not know how, and you may not know when, but God's done it before and HE'LL do it again. Thank You, Lord.

> *Weeping may endure for a night, but joy comes in the morning. (Psalm 30:5)*

Praise God. Besides, God has all those tears in a bottle as healing medicine. Repent, forgive, bless and go on, then streams of refreshing will come for YOU. It's His plan. Besides, tests don't last forever, just until we pass them. Then we get promoted to the next one.

It's the onward and upward plan, UNLESS we choose to reject and resist the chastening and warnings of God. THEN we've signed up for the how low can you go plan. But, praise God, there's a light at the top of that hole, so look UP. Jesus paid the price for our sins. He bought our forgiveness. We just have to quit rebelling, quit defending, quit justifying our sin, and call it what God does, SIN. Repent and CHANGE. *1 John 1:5b-10* is very clear:

> *God is light, and in Him there is no darkness at all. If we say that we have fellowship with Him and yet walk in the darkness, we lie and do not practice the truth; but if we walk in the light as He Himself is in the light, we have fellowship with one another, and the blood of Jesus His Son cleanses us from ALL sin. If we say that we have no sin, we are deceiving ourselves, and the truth is not in us. If we confess our sins, He is faithful and righteous to forgive us our sins and to cleanse us from all unrighteousness. If we say that we have not sinned, we make Him a liar, and His word is not in us*

Situations either have the favor and blessings of God upon them, OR He is frustrating man's plan just to let us know that **HE is GOD and We are NOT!** We will do it HIS way for HIS blessing. Life and death is set before you today, the curse or the blessing. *(See Deuteronomy 6-8)* We can take God easy or we can take Him hard, but how many more laps do we want to take around the wilderness? (Hebrews 3) Choose LIFE.

WHERE YOUR TREASURE IS
There is your heart also

Put your money where your mouth is

GOD owns it ALL. That's the beginning and the end of it. The tithing issue is non-negotiable and is 10% for the children of God. This principle is all through the Bible. You will be blessed if you obey and cursed if you don't. God makes things REAL simple so that even a child can't miss Him and His ways.

> *Will a man rob God? Yet you are robbing Me. But you say, "How have we robbed Thee?" "In tithes and offerings. You are cursed with a curse, for you are robbing Me, the whole nation of you. Bring the whole tithe into the storehouse, so that there may be food in My house, and test Me now in this," says the Lord of hosts, "if I will not open for you the windows of heaven and pour out for you a blessing until it overflows. Then I will rebuke the devourer for you, so that it may not destroy the fruits of the ground; nor will your vine in the field cast its grapes," says the Lord of hosts. "And all the nations will call you blessed, for you shall be a delightful land.". . .So you will again distinguish between the righteous and the wicked, between one who serves God and one who does not serve Him." (Malachi 3:8-12,18)*

Other scriptures are: *Genesis 28:22, Leviticus 27:30, Numbers 18:26,28, Deuteronomy 12:17, 14:22, Proverbs 11:24, Luke 18:12,* and *Hebrews 7:1-10.* The deal is, it's ALL God's.

> *But you shall remember the Lord your God, for it is He who is giving you power to make wealth, that He may confirm His covenant which He swore to your fathers. (Deuteronomy 8:18)*

The principle of choosing the blessing versus the curse spoken of in *Deuteronomy 5-8* is, we're blessed IF we do what

GOD says and we're cursed if we don't. If you're not walking in obedience to God through His Word and under HIS covering of protection and blessing, the devil can steal anything he wants from you and yours, whenever he wants.

Case in point - a member of my family was not tithing, and we warned him that he was fair game for the devil stealing anything he had because he was not under God's umbrella of protection. Several weeks later when he called to say his car had been broken into and his stereo stolen, I asked, "Are you tithing yet?"

"No."

A few weeks later, another call came - His CAR had been stolen.

"Are you tithing yet?"

"No."

"Enjoy your Nike's because that's the last dime you'll see from this house."

The Lord had dealt with us about throwing His money away. You're free to make your choices, but not free from the consequences of those choices.

> *Do not give what is holy to dogs, and do not throw your pearls before swine, lest they trample them under their feet, and turn and tear you to pieces. (Matthew 7:6)*

Oh well, we can take God easy or we can take Him hard - but **GOD IS GOD and We are NOT!** He protects what's HIS and even tells us to test Him concerning this issue. If, however, you are stealing HIS tenth, please don't share your sob stories with me, for all I'll ask you is, "ARE YOU TITHING?" When you say that you're not, I'll have to assure you that my prayers wouldn't work. Read Malachi again. Repent and change. Obedience is always a choice. I've never known anyone who started tithing out of their abundance in the beginning. But when you take that first step, God blesses it, and then takes you into HIS abundance. I'd rather have 90% of everything than 100% of nothing.

> *Beloved I pray that you may prosper and be in good health, even as your soul prospers. (3 John 2)*

We are all either blessed or not, dependent on whether we're in obedience or rebellion to God's laws. Ignorance is NO excuse, JUST READ THE BOOK AND DO WHAT IT SAYS.

My people are destroyed for lack of knowledge. (Hosea 4:6a)

For even though they knew God, they did not honor Him as God, or give thanks; but they became futile in their speculations, and their foolish heart was darkened. (Romans 1:21)

Why not throw out all those magazines and books until you've read the Word of God five or six times, cover to cover. The Word is TRUE and it will change your life and your circumstances. Are you ready?

For the WORD is living and active and sharper than any two-edged sword, and piercing as far as the division of soul and spirit, of both joints and marrow, and able to judge the thoughts and intentions of the heart. (Hebrews 4:12)

Thy word have I treasured in my heart, that I may not sin against Thee. (Psalm 119:11)

In it is God's solution for every problem you're facing. Let's walk it God's way and He'll fight for us. Let's be faithful in little, so we'll be made ruler over much *(Matthew 25:14-30)*.

Also, a word to you prayer warriors. Don't bother God with prayers that you have the resources to answer. How easy and religious to say, "I'll pray for you." NO, brother or sister, that's not how it works in the body. If you can answer the prayer, Jesus said, "Freely you received, freely give." *(Matthew 10:8b)*

That's pretty simple, isn't it? Then in *1 John 3:17:*

But whoever has the world's goods, and beholds his brother in need and closes his heart against him, how does the love of God abide in him?

It's ALL God's. So we just need to find out what HE wants done with everything He's given us. You have two cars and see that your brother has none? Well, pray BROTHER, and see if that second car belongs to him.

> *Give and it shall be given unto you, good measure, pressed down, shaken together, running over, they will pour into your lap. For by your standard of measure it will be measured to you in return. (Luke 6:38)*

First need has first claim, regardless of whose house it's in. Shall we walk what we talk, Christians?

Once, I was in Israel with a Bible Institute group, listening to a pastor share his powerful testimony of leaving it all to follow Jesus. After he finished, the leader of our group responded with, "Let's pray for this brother."

OH, PLEASE. This man had just finished sharing his story of leaving a prosperous Los Angeles law practice to go to Jerusalem and pastor an Arab church (for $200.00 a month) and we're going to PRAY for him? GOD WAS NOT PLEASED.

The Holy Spirit prompted me to ask, "Why don't we just put our money where our mouth is and give Brother Milad EVERYTHING in our pockets?" It seemed everyone in the group had plenty of money for what they'd wanted.

Never had I felt so intensely the wrath of the religious.

Jesus taught in *Matthew 25:34-46*:

> *Then the King will say to those on His right, "Come, you who are blessed of My Father, inherit the kingdom prepared for you from the foundation of the world. For I was hungry, and you gave Me something to eat; I was thirsty, and you gave Me drink; I was a stranger, and you invited Me in; naked, and you clothed Me; I was sick and you visited Me; I was in prison and you came to Me."*
>
> *Then the righteous will answer Him, saying, "Lord, when did we see You hungry, and feed You, or thirsty, and give You drink? And when did we see You a stranger, and invite You in, or naked, and clothe You? And when did we see You sick, or in prison, and come to You?" And the King will answer and say to them, "Truly I say to you, to the extent that you did it to one of these brothers of Mine, even the least of them, you did it to ME."*

Where Your Treasure Is

Then He will also say to those on His left, "Depart from Me, accursed ones, into the eternal fire which has been prepared for the devil and his angels; for I was hungry and you gave Me nothing to eat; I was thirsty, and you gave Me nothing to drink; I was a stranger, and you did not invite Me in; naked, and you did not clothe Me; sick, and in prison, and you did not visit Me." Then they themselves also will answer, saying, "Lord, when did we see You hungry, or thirsty, or a stranger, or naked, or sick, or in prison, and did not take care of You?" Then He will answer them, saying, "Truly I say to you, to the extent that you did not do it to one of the least of these, you did not do it to Me." And these will go away into eternal punishment, but the righteous into eternal life.

Another issue is creative financing. When Mikala and I moved to our apartment, we noticed there were no overhead lights, so we asked God for some. He told us to go down to the trash room. We went and...there were our lamps. (Ditto for a bed, vacuum, luggage, etc.) That was a high class, anointed trash room, and the angels were always making deliveries. We'd just pray and the original owners would turn stuff loose.

The wealth of the wicked IS stored up for the righteous. (Job 27:16-17, Psalm 105:44, Isaiah 23:18, 60:5-9 and Ecclesiastes 2:26)

When Nick died, God told me to sell his Jeep. The following four years, I had no car of my own, however, God always provided me with one to use. When my mother went to be with Jesus, she left her car for ME. HALLELUJAH.

We've never seen the righteous forsaken, or their seed begging for bread. (Psalm 37:25)

IT WORKS. God's word is true. Try it and you'll see. Concerning giving, write in the anointing you want, add it to your tithes and offerings, and give it each week.

Give, and it will be given unto you; good measure, pressed down, shaken together, running over, they will pour into your lap. For by your standard of measure it will be measured to you in return. (Luke 6:38)

When the church really gets it, we won't be begging for money. It will be as in Moses' day, when he was told to build the Tabernacle in *Exodus 36:5-7:*

> *And they said to Moses, "The people are bringing much more than enough for the construction work which the Lord commanded us to perform." So Moses issued a command, and a proclamation was circulated throughout the camp, saying, "Let neither man nor woman any longer perform work for the contributions of the sanctuary." Thus the people were restrained from bringing any more. For the material they had was sufficient and more than enough for all the work, to perform it.*

This also happened in *1 Kings 8:64* when the altar was too small to hold all the burnt offerings. Hallelujah. God is the God of MORE than enough for His children. Remember, it's ALL His. Let's ask HIM how HE would like HIS money spent. The great thing is that God can set up our finances so we can live on 10% and seed 90% into HIS kingdom.

> *"For My thoughts are not your thoughts, neither are your ways My ways," declares the Lord. "For as the heavens are higher than the earth, so are My ways higher than your ways, and My thoughts than your thoughts." (Isaiah 55:8-9)*

GOD IS GOD and We are NOT! He owns it ALL and is looking for people to steward His funds through for His purposes and HIS honor and glory. Will we be found *"faithful in little, so we will be entrusted with much?"* (Matthew 25:14-30) We aren't going to take it with us but we will give an account. So let's make God proud of His kids.

FAITH

Or...THE BATTLE IS THE LORD'S

God sums up the walk, *"and without faith, it is impossible to please Him, for he who comes to God must believer that He is, and that He is a rewarder of those who seek Him."* (Hebrews 11:6)

With that as the foundation you can have a TOP-of-the-day everyday -- Trust, Obey and Praise God.

It seemed that EVERYONE was coming against King Jehoshaphat in *2 Chronicles 20:1-13,* and he was afraid, so he:

Turned his attention to seek the Lord; and proclaimed a fast throughout all Judah. So Judah gathered together to seek help from the Lord. . .and he said, "O Lord, the God of our fathers, art Thou not God in the heavens? And art Thou not ruler over all the kingdoms of the nations? Power and might are in Thy hand so that no one can stand against Thee."

(In modern terms -- Lord, You are God, HELP.)

That's the TRUST part, he's praying and trusting God to answer.

The OBEY part comes next in verses 14-18:

Then in the midst of the assembly, the Spirit of the Lord came upon Jahaziel. . .and he said, "Listen, all Judah and the inhabitants of Jerusalem and King Jehoshaphat: thus says the Lord to you, 'Do not fear or be dismayed because of this great multitude, for the battle is not yours but GOD'S. Tomorrow go down against them. . .you need not fight in this battle; station yourselves, stand and see the salvation of the Lord on your behalf, O Judah and Jerusalem. Do not fear or be dismayed; tomorrow go out to face them, for the Lord is with you.'"

God gave the game plan for this battle and assured them the battle wasn't theirs, but His. That's how it is child of the Most High God. And after that word, the King went into the PRAISE part (verses 18-19):

> And Jehoshaphat bowed his head with his face to the ground, and all Judah and the inhabitants of Jerusalem fell down before the Lord, worshipping the Lord. And the Levites. . .stood up to praise the Lord, God of Israel with a very loud voice.

The culmination of TRUST, OBEY and PRAISE is the overcoming and winning that follows in verses 20-25, a textbook case that children of God would do well to follow:

> (OBEY) And they rose early in the morning. . .and when they went out, Jehoshaphat stood and said, "Listen to me, O Judah and inhabitants of Jerusalem, put your trust in the Lord your God, and you will be established. Put your trust in His prophets and succeed." (TRUST)

> (PRAISE) He appointed those who sang to the Lord and those who praised Him in holy attire, as they went out before the army and said, "Give thanks to the Lord, for His lovingkindness is everlasting." And when they began singing and praising, the Lord set ambushes. . . .For the sons of Ammon and Moab rose up against the inhabitants of Mount Seir destroying them completely, and when they had finished with the inhabitants of Seir, they helped to destroy one another.

See verses 24-25, for the final tally in a battle that God fights:

> And behold, they were corpses lying on the ground, and no one had escaped. And when Jehoshaphat and his people came to take their spoil, they found much among them, including goods, garments, and valuable things which they took for themselves, more than they could carry. And they were three days taking the spoil because there was so much.

The reaction of God's children to their Father's victory follows in verses 27-30:

> *And every man. . .returned with JOY, for the Lord had made them to rejoice over their enemies. And they came to Jerusalem with harps, lyres, and trumpets to the house of the Lord. And the dread of God was on all the kingdoms of the lands when they heard that the Lord had fought against the enemies of Israel. So the kingdom of Jehoshaphat was at peace, for his GOD gave him rest on all sides.*

That's rather spectacular. Not only does God NOT lose - BUT also He makes your enemies so afraid that you have peace on ALL sides.

> *When a man's ways are pleasing to the Lord, He makes even his enemies to be at peace with him. (Proverbs 16:7)*

Remember David and Goliath? God made that giant SO big, David couldn't miss him. David knew God's ways:

> *"You come to me with a sword, a spear, and a javelin, but I come to you in the name of the Lord of hosts, the God of the armies of Israel, whom you have taunted. This day, the Lord will deliver you into my hands, and I will strike you down and remove your head from you. . .that all the Earth may know that there is a GOD in Israel, and that all this assembly may know that the Lord does not deliver by sword or by spear; for the battle is the Lord's and He will give you into our hands." Then it happened when the Philistine rose and came and drew near to meet David, that David RAN quickly toward the battle. . .* (The rest is HISTORY). . .*Thus David prevailed over the Philistine with a sling and a stone, and he struck the Philistine and killed him; but there was no sword in David's hand. (1 Samuel 17:45-50)*

As David had been faithful in little, he would be given much. Are we being faithful over our little? If not, we should not expect much. How we treat the things that belong to others determines if we are ready for blessings of our own. The Lord was watching, during those four years as I drove other people's cars, to see how I took care of them - before He gave me one with my name on the title. HALLELUJAH. Renters, are you treating that home as you'd want someone to treat yours?

And just as you want people to treat you, treat them in the same way. (Luke 6:31)

Along the lines of faithfulness - sometimes when praying for people, God says that He's not going to heal them instantly, or they would run off and leave Him again. Self-pity, control and manipulation, murmuring and complaining can also be obstacles to healing.

When I was flat on my back and all I could do was look up, God got my attention concerning many things that I would never have taken time to hear before. So often it's not about our healing, it's about God's good purpose in our lives.

Once, when praying for a teen-ager's deaf ears to open, God showed me the blessing side of it. Her ears had never been defiled by the world. Likewise, several times with the blind, their eyes had never been defiled through sight. *(See Matthew 5:27-30.)* God's ways are so much higher than ours are. YES, I believe in healing. I'm a cripple who walks today - God did it. Praise to the LIVING GOD, the curse of muscular dystrophy is broken off my life. The day after I ran home healed, my insurance agent was coming over to discuss my pre-existing condition limitations for medical insurance. Well, being a brother in the faith, I told him that he didn't need to worry about that - GOD HAD HEALED ME. What a test. The next test was the Church ski trip that took place the following week. For the last few years my ski trips always meant pain and injury. However, this year would be different - I WAS HEALED.

Another test of faith came the night before we were to hit the slopes. God said, "Tell them I healed you and you'll be giving lessons on the slopes tomorrow." GOD IS FAITHFUL...and I DID.

A sad commentary on healing is that some folks would rather see a person on crutches than believe and receive that GOD still heals TODAY. So remember to stand firm in what the Lord has said. Believe by faith in healing or walk in doubt and fear. What you look at you will have. Besides, the devil is a liar, let God be exalted. Whose report will we believe? The WORD says, *"For by His stripes you ARE healed."* (Isaiah 53:5) BELIEVE AND RECEIVE. When you believe, you finish with prayers of thanksgiving. God isn't deaf, and when He speaks, never doubt it. But, God always says "IF" – *"If you abide in Me and My word abides in you, ask what you will and it shall be done for you."* (John 15:7)

> *Take care, brethren, lest there should be in any one of you an evil, unbelieving heart, in falling away from the living God. But encourage one another day after day. . . lest any one of you be hardened by the deceitfulness of sin. For we have become partakers of Christ, if we hold fast the beginning of our assurance firm until the end. . . And so we see, that they were not able to enter because of unbelief. Therefore, let us fear lest, while a promise remains of entering His rest, any one of you should seem to have come short of it.* (Hebrews 3:12-4:1)

God promises us a place of rest, IF, we will believe. I ask God to cleanse you of all clutter, confusion and distractions and in His mercy walk you into the place of rest, through faith, that He has for His children today.

As He asked in *Genesis 3:9*, *"Adam, Adam, where are you?"* The Father is still looking for, and calling His children, to come:

> *Come to Me all who are weary and heavy-laden, and I will give you rest. Take My yoke upon you, and learn from Me, for I am gentle and humble in heart; and YOU SHALL FIND REST FOR YOUR SOULS. For My yoke is easy, and My load is light.* (Matthew 11:28-30)

Let's jump into that great faith chapter of *Hebrews 11*. Read about the price the old-timers paid to heed the call of God, to be mentioned in the WORD, and to encourage us to go forth.

GOD IS GOD and We are NOT!

> *By faith, Moses. . .choosing rather to endure ill-treatment with the people of God, than to enjoy the passing pleasures of sin; considering the reproach of Christ greater riches than the treasures of Egypt; for he was looking to the reward. By faith he left Egypt, not fearing the wrath of the king; for he endured, as seeing Him who is unseen. (Hebrews 11:24-27)*

God has promised. He's done it before and He'll do it again. Hold on in faith and know that what He's said is true. He will take you forward, not backwards. He has a plan and is going to work it all out. Receive those promises in His Word, because they are ALL for you, today. Put your name in the blanks.

> *Jesus speaks, "And from the days of John the Baptist until now the kingdom of heaven suffers violence, and violent men take it by force." (Matthew 11:12)*

And they DO. When you have suffered violence, you have qualified to take it back by force. Only David could use Goliath's sword *(1 Samuel 21:9).*

"God, I know You are true, that You have plans for me, and that everything You have promised will come to pass."

Let God handle those situations you can't while you just look up in hope, knowing that He will take you THROUGH. Take it right where you are. God's a GOOD God. He's a redeeming God and the past is past. Keep your focus on the bigger picture, the God who is sovereign and Lord of ALL, or not at all. The man who has only God to look to can do ALL things and never fail. Attempt something so impossible that without God, it's destined to fail and then hang on to the hem of His garment and He WILL pull you THROUGH.

MY COLORS WILL BE CLEAR

I am part of the fellowship of the unashamed.
The die has been cast. I have stepped over the line.
The decision has been made. I am a disciple of JESUS.
I won't look back, let up, slow down, back away or be still.
My past is redeemed, my present makes sense,
my future is secure.
I'm finished and done with low living, with slight walking,
with small planning, with smooth knees, with colorless
dreams, with tamed visions, with mundane talking,
with chintzy giving and dwarfed goals.
I no longer need prosperity, position, promotions, and plaudits
or popularity. I don't have to be right, first, tops,
recognized, praised, regarded or rewarded.
I now live by presence, learn by faith, walk by patience,
lift by prayer, and labor by power.
My face is set, my gait is fast, my goal is heaven,
my road is narrow, my way is rough, my companions few,
my Guide reliable, my mission clear.
I can't be bought, compromised, detoured,
lured away, turned back, deluded, or delayed.
I will not flinch in the face of sacrifice, hesitate in the
presence of the adversary, negotiate at the table of the enemy,
ponder at the pool of popularity.
I won't give up, shut up, or let up, until I have stayed up,
stored up, prayed up, paid up, and preached up
the cause of CHRIST.
I must go till HE comes, give till I drop, proclaim till all know,
and work till HE stops me. And when HE comes for His
own...HE will have no problem recognizing me

FOR MY COLORS WILL BE CLEAR

Found in the pocket of a man martyred for Christ in South Africa

PASTORS and MINISTERS...

YOU CAN TAKE THEM TO WHERE YOU ARE

Pastors:

A word of warning...God is raising up some David's among us who ARE God's anointed. They are out there slaying giants. When they show up in your church, take care that you don't spear them to death.
Who was God's anointed, Saul or David? Sometimes we don't know for sure. Let's not kill all those up and coming shepherd boys who HAVE had the oil poured on them. God is going to write this last chapter according to HIS specifications - not ours. Let's just line up behind the King of kings and Lord of lords - doing things HIS way lest we also in jealousy, anger and hatred wind up consulting a witch and dying before our time - because WE no longer hear from GOD.
God is NOT playing, and we'd better be open to Him in whatever form HE chooses to come - lest we also miss our day of visitation because we chose the stiff-necked, hard-hearted ways that led the Pharisees to hang our Messiah on a tree. No, the sheep won't be perfect, and sometimes they make a mess, but it's not the shepherd that bears lambs, but the sheep. Let's all be a part of GOD'S Body - arms, legs, feet and hands. Remember, there's only one head - CHRIST JESUS, our Lord.
Jesus stood before Pilate and uttered not a word in His own defense. If God called you, HE will keep you. We must have nothing to protect and nothing to defend. **GOD IS GOD and We are NOT!**
Pastor Gene Edwards may have said it best in <u>A Tale of Three Kings</u>, speaking of David:

" 'It is better I be defeated, even killed, than to learn the ways of...a Saul, or the ways of an Absalom. The kingdom is not that valuable. Let him have it, if that be the Lord's will. I repeat; I shall not learn the ways of either Sauls or Absaloms. No man knows his own heart. I certainly don't know mine. Only God does. Shall I defend my little realm in the name of God? Shall I throw spears, and plot and divide...and kill men's spirits if not their bodies...to protect my empire? I did not lift a finger to be made King, nor to preserve a kingdom; even the Kingdom of God. GOD PUT ME HERE. It is not my responsibility to take, or keep authority. Do you not realize, it may be His will for these things to take place? I suspect that, if HE chose, God could protect and keep the kingdom even now. After all, IT IS HIS KINGDOM. In either case, I shall raise no hand. Wouldn't I look a little strange trying to stay in control when God was desiring that I fall? I will not fight to be king or to remain king.

May God come tonight and take the throne, the kingship and. . . ' David's voice faltered, 'and His anointing from me. I seek His will, not His power. I repeat, I desire His will more than I desire a position of leadership. Today I shall give circumstances ample space for this untelling God of ours to be found out. I know of no other way to bring about such an extraordinary event except by doing NOTHING. The throne is not mine. Not to have, not to take, not to protect, and not to keep.

I shall leave the city. The throne is the Lord's. So is the kingdom. I will not hinder God. No obstacle, no activity on my part lies in the space between God and His will. He has no hindrance to prevent Him from His will. If I am not to be King, our God will find no difficulties in making Absalom to be Israel's king. Now it is possible. GOD SHALL BE GOD.' The true king turned and walked quietly out of the throne room, out of the palace, out of the city. . .And he walked. . .into the bosoms of all men whose hearts are pure."

> *God left him alone to test him, that He might know all that was in his heart. (2 Chronicles 32:31b)*

It seems that God is always testing our hearts, as the Lord did Moses' in *Exodus 32:10-14:*

> *Now then let Me alone, that My anger may burn against them, and that I may destroy them; and I will make of you a great nation.* But Moses jumped in with: *"O Lord, why doth Thine anger burn against Thy people whom Thou hast brought out from the land of Egypt. . .turn from Thy burning anger and change Thy mind about*

doing harm to Thy people.". . .So the Lord changed His mind.

You really are a man or woman of God when you'd rather protect God's image than your own. The spoken word that God had given Moses stood in the way. God won't go against His Word. Moses had a shepherd's heart. Daniel, a true prophet, said, *"Keep your gifts." (Daniel 5:17)* Moses became the most humble man when he stood in the gap for God's children.

Will we be a donkey to save a Baalam's life even when we get beat three times and would be killed if the guy had a sword? BUT Baalam LIVED. Sometimes, there's just no thanks for being a servant of God; only the reward that people live and not die. ALL who will may come. May we be those watchmen on the wall so there's no blood on our hands. Let's not protect people from their God, who alone can save them, so they will like us.

Elihu said, "Let me now be partial to no one; nor flatter any man. For I do not know how to flatter, else my Maker would take me away." (Job 32:21-22)

We have to fearlessly say what God is saying, for one day we will give account.

I, even I, am HE who comforts you. Who are you that you are afraid of man who dies, and of the son of man who is made like grass; that you have forgotten the Lord your Maker? (Isaiah 51:12-13)

Let not many of you become teachers, my brethren, knowing that as such, we shall incur a stricter judgment. (James 3:1)

Also the admonition from *Hebrews 13:17:*

"Obey your leaders, and submit to them, for they keep watch over your souls, as those who will give an account."

Pastors,

To whom much is given, much is required. (Luke 12:48)

May it never be said of us:

Those who are sickly you have not strengthened, the diseased you have not healed, the broken you have not bound up, the scattered you have not brought back, nor have you sought for the lost; but with force and severity you have dominated them. And they were scattered for lack of a shepherd, and they became food for every beast

Pastors and Ministers

of the field and were scattered. . . .My flock has become a prey, My flock has even become food for all the beasts of the field for lack of a shepherd, and My shepherds did not search for My flock, but rather the shepherds fed themselves and did not feed My flock; therefore, you shepherds, hear the word of the Lord: Thus says the Lord God, "Behold, I am against the shepherds, and I shall demand My sheep from them and make them cease from feeding sheep. So the shepherds will not feed themselves anymore, but I shall deliver My flock from their mouth, that they may not be food for them." (Ezekiel 34:2-10)

God is firing shepherds like the ones mentioned above. During a revival with an international evangelist, a word was given to the pastor that God wanted to heal marriages. It seemed there were 33 couples that GOD wanted to restore. Neither the evangelist nor the pastor would minister the word of the Lord to the couples. The next night, God said, "Last night, we lost 13 of those couples." The word still was not received nor given. After the service, the evangelist suffered a severe heart attack with complications and spent six months in the hospital, during which time, his wife suffered a nervous breakdown. God isn't playing, we will do it HIS way or WE will be fired, and he will chose another. God was very clear to Elijah in *1 Kings 19:*

Go and anoint your replacement. . . .Yet I will leave 7,000 in Israel, all the knees that have not bowed to Baal and every mouth that has not kissed him.

ALL things hidden will come to light. Regardless of our position in the eyes of man, we MUST keep our house in order and be willing to receive God in whatever form He comes. God is exposing secret sin. How can you say you love God when you're not loving the spouse He gave you?

Lord, how is it that when You write Ichabod *(1 Samuel 19:21-22)* and depart - the show still goes on? May it never be.

The level of your ministry, its holiness, and anointing, is directly related to your home ground. Don't put on a show at church when you've deserted that family God's given you. Don't blame it on God. It is GOD'S church and YOUR family. God has lots of ministers, however, your wife has only ONE husband and your children have only ONE dad. The responsibility of priest in your family is YOURS alone. If you raise GOD'S sheep right, they will birth the lambs and you'll only have to shepherd GOD'S flock. Misplaced priorities will get you in serious trouble. Those husband scriptures apply to preachers also - so come out from behind that cloak and love your wife as Christ loves the church. Who else can set that standard for the flock? And the way YOU walk, they'll walk. God has given you your wife as a helpmate, a best friend to talk to, and someone to keep you from pride. So, watch those steps at home and away from home, because God surely is - and we will give account to Him. Let's have some good scores for the HOME TEAM.

Next is the issue of respect of persons and people pleasing:

Paul said, "The Lord is my helper, I will not be afraid. What shall man do to me?" (Hebrews 13:6)

Jesus said, "But do not be called Rabbi; for One is your Teacher, and you are all brothers. And do not call anyone on earth your father; for One is your Father, He who is in heaven. And do not be called leaders; for One is your Leader, that is, Christ. But the greatest among you shall be your servant. And whoever exalts himself shall be humbled; and whoever humbles himself shall be exalted." (Matthew 23:8-12)

God is raising up ministers at the grassroots level, almost an under-ground type, EVERYWHERE. God's kids are taking the land for Him, and through HIM - people that probably wouldn't be allowed behind most pulpits. Isn't that how Jesus and His disciples had to walk? And 2,000 years later, His disciples are still doing the stuff. Sometimes you just find it easier to be about the Father's business at the local Red Lobster than in the synagogues and churches. *Jesus said, "Go to the highways and byways and compel them to come in." (Luke 14:23)* ARE WE? Because if we aren't, God still has 7,000 who will take our place of calling, and march forward at HIS bidding to go and do His will, HIS way. **GOD IS GOD and We are NOT!** His is the Master's plan and there will be no cheap imitations.

God is looking for a people who will say what He says, drawing no attention to themselves by jokes, or half-truths, etc.

James 5:12 admonishes, "Let your yes be yes, and your no, no; so that you may not fall under judgment."

Pastors and Ministers 125

> Jesus said, "And I say to you, that every careless word that men shall speak, they shall render account for it in the day of judgment. For by your words you shall be justified, and by your words you shall be condemned." (Matthew 12:36-37)
> I testify to everyone who hears the words of the prophecy of this book: if anyone adds to them, God shall add to him the plagues which are written in this book; and if anyone takes away from the words of the book of this prophecy, God shall take away his part from the tree of life and from the holy city. (Revelation 22:18-19)

Samuel had a 100% anointing BECAUSE he just said what God said, adding nothing of himself to it. Will we die to let the King speak through us? Will we say what God is saying regardless of the consequences? Please man or God? We must choose this day who we will serve; nickels and noses or a HOLY, and righteous God?

> Paul said in 1 Corinthians 2:1-5, "And when I came to you, brethren, I did not come with superiority of speech or of wisdom, proclaiming to you the testimony of God. For I determined to know nothing among you except Jesus Christ, and Him crucified. And I was with you in weakness and in fear and in much trembling. And my message and my preaching were not in persuasive words of wisdom, but in demonstration of the Spirit and of power, that your faith should not rest on the wisdom of men, but on the power of God."

Will we in the face of ALL opposition rely on the Holy Spirit to move THROUGH us, to will and to do God's good purpose? Will we trust the God who called us to be faithful to complete that good work He began? (1Thessalonians 5:24)

> Jesus said in John 3:8, "The wind blows where it wishes and you hear the sound of it, but do not know where it comes from and where it is going; so is everyone who is born of the Spirit."

Likewise in *Numbers 9:23* concerning the cloud guiding them:

> *At the command of the Lord they camped, and at the command of the Lord, they set out; they kept the Lord's charge, according to the command of the Lord through Moses.*

Moses certainly had God's call on his life. He talked with God and God showed up on his behalf. How would you like to walk close enough to God that He would swallow up your enemies? (See *Numbers 16:21-44.*) We can, IF we will pay the price to WALK with GOD. Moses walked with God, then gave the people what he got on that mountain. Let's go and do likewise.

Pastors, I ask God to protect you, defend you, make His face to shine upon you and give you, PEACE. That He take you back into that special place of abode you knew so well before the torrents of the ministry came crashing in upon you. Let it all go - **GOD IS GOD and We are NOT!** I ask God to set you free from the religious games people play and to allow all things hidden to come to light. To guide and direct your steps as you lead HIS sheep. That you will hear clearly the Shepherd's voice with no distractions, clutter nor confusion.

That God send His Holy Spirit to guide, comfort and lead you into ALL truth. I pray for God's anointing upon your life and ministry to take HIS children to the throne. That the Lord allow the same fire that fell on Mount Carmel to come and burn out everything in your church, life and ministry that is displeasing to Him, that blocks the view to Jesus, or would take the glory that is His alone. Let's unite and go tell a lost and dying world that the King of kings and Lord of lords is the solution for their lives and that He is returning. Let's love the brethren and be about the Father's business.

Blessings, servants of the Most High GOD.

P.S. For any of you sheep who just happened into this chapter...
Some words of wisdom. Think the best of, pray for, thank God for and support that man or woman of God who's watching over

Pastors and Ministers

your soul. Paul said, *"Follow me, as I follow Christ."* If you see areas that don't line up with the word of God - talk to GOD about that situation. If you cannot submit, ask God where He would have you serve. REMEMBER: TOUCH NOT GOD'S ANOINTED. *(See 1 Samuel 24:6; 26:9,16,23 and Numbers 16.)* IF God didn't call you there, you can't stay. IF He did, you can't leave. So build up and don't tear down. Besides, just how many souls have you led to Jesus today? Are you praying and fasting more than the man or woman of God you are finding fault with? If not, it would behoove you to shut your mouth, lest leprosy come upon you also. (See *Numbers 12*) AMEN. And thank God that you don't have the awesome responsibility before God that he or she does. Be blessed, children of the Most High God, it's onward and upward. Take up your cross and call and go forth to do what God has called you to do to build up the Body.

Behold, I am coming quickly, and My reward is with Me, to render to every man according to what he has done. (Revelation 22:12)

Let's be about the Father's business, uplifting the brethren, until He returns.

May God richly and abundantly bless you and yours.

Beloved, I pray that in all respects you may prosper and be in good health, just as your soul prospers. (3 John 2)